THE GOD IN YOU BIBLE STUDY SERIES

LEADER'S GUIDE

A Bible Study by

Churches Alive!

MINISTERING TO THE CHURCHES OF THE WORLD
600 Meridian Avenue, Suite 200
San Jose, California 95126-3427

Published by

NAVPRESS
BRINGING TRUTH TO LIFE
NavPress Publishing Group
P.O. Box 35001, Colorado Springs, Colorado 80935

Ninth printing, 1994

Cover illustration: Catherine Kanner

Unless otherwise identified, all Scripture quo-
tations in this publication are taken from the
HOLY BIBLE: NEW INTERNATIONAL VER-
SION® (NIV®). Copyright © 1973, 1978, 1984
by International Bible Society. Used by permis-
sion of Zondervan Publishing House. All rights
reserved.

Printed in the United States of America

Because we share kindred aims for helping local churches fulfill Christ's Great Commission to "go and make disciples," NavPress and Churches Alive have joined efforts on certain strategic publishing projects that are intended to bring effective disciplemaking resources into the service of the local church.

For more than a decade, Churches Alive has teamed up with churches of all denominations to establish vigorous disciplemaking ministries. At the same time, NavPress has focused on publishing Bible studies, books, and other resources that have grown out of The Navigators' fifty years of disciplemaking experience.

Now, together, we're working to offer special products like this one that are designed to stimulate a deeper, more fruitful commitment to Christ in the local gatherings of His Church.

The GOD IN YOU Bible Study Series *was written by Russ Korth, Ron Wormser, Jr., and Ron Wormser, Sr., of Churches Alive. Many individuals from both Churches Alive and NavPress contributed greatly in bringing this project to publication.*

Contents

Rich!

Powerful!

Changed!

Fulfilled!

Celebrate!

About the Author

In your hand you have just one item of a *wide range* of discipling helps, authored and developed by Churches Alive with *one overall, church-centered, biblical concept* in mind: GROWING BY DISCIPLING!

Convinced that the local church is the heart of God's plan for the world, a number of Christian leaders joined in 1973 to form Churches Alive. They saw the need for someone to work hand-in-hand with local churches to help them develop fruitful discipleship ministries.

Today, the ministry of Churches Alive has grown to include personal consulting assistance to church leaders, a variety of discipleship books and materials, and training conferences for clergy and laypeople. These methods and materials have proven effective in churches large and small of over 45 denominations.From their commitment and experience in church ministry, Churches Alive developed the Growing by Discipling plan to help you

- minister to people at their levels of maturity.
- equip people for ministry.
- generate mature leaders.
- perpetuate quality.
- balance growth and outreach.

Every part of Growing by Discipling works together in harmony to meet the diverse needs of people — from veteran church members to the newly awakened in Christ. This discipling approach allows you to integrate present fruitful ministries and create additional ones through the new leaders you develop.

This concept follows Christ's disciplemaking example by helping you to meet people at their points of need. Then, you help them build their dependence on God so they experience His love and power. Finally, you equip them to reach out to others in a loving, effective, and balanced ministry of evangelism and helping hands.Headquartered in San Bernardino, California, with staff across the United States and in Europe, Churches Alive continues to expand its ministry in North America and overseas.

Introduction

GOD IN YOU helps you and your group explore a topic by closely examining a Bible passage.

FOCUS ON MAJOR TEACHINGS AND APPLICATIONS

As a group leader, your primary concern should be guiding your group to understand and apply the biblical teaching on a given topic. This means that some weeks, interesting and important parts of the study passage may not receive much attention. This will not be a problem if you remind your group from time to time that you are looking for major teachings and applications.

Each chapter is designed for personal study at home followed by one hour of group discussion. Do not spend more than one week per chapter, or you will find some group members demotivated by the slow pace. Also, if the members do not have a new chapter to complete each week, they will not establish a regular habit of study. Remember, it is more important to keep people enthused than to exhaustively cover the passage or topic. Expect many gems of biblical truth to go undiscovered.

LEARN NEW BIBLE STUDY SKILLS

This study series also helps people learn how to examine a Bible passage on their own. They learn this skill subtly as they work through the chapters. The questions acquaint them with different approaches to Bible study. After using these approaches a number of times, the skills become a way of life for studying other passages.

FOLLOW A PROVEN APPROACH

You can help keep the study relevant by keeping in mind the three major steps for studying any passage in the Bible: observation, interpretation, and application. Though you can begin using these tools right away, you cannot master them in a lifetime.

OBSERVATION is the art of seeing what is in a passage without attempting to determine the correct meaning.

INTERPRETATION is the process of determining the correct meaning of the observation(s). Many books have been written about this process. There is no simple way to tell you how to interpret correctly, but most people begin with this basic rule: Interpret the Bible in the same way you interpret any other book. If the common meaning makes sense, seek no other sense. If and when you need more help on the proper ways to interpret, consult other resources (such as your pastor and Bible reference books).

APPLICATION is relating Bible truth to your life. God gave us His Word to help us live within His design and desires. Studying the Bible just to acquire knowledge is like eating food without digesting it. It does not produce the benefits for your life that God intends.

As you explore the questions in each chapter, you will notice they emphasize all three of these aspects of study. Generally speaking, the early exercises in a chapter will focus on observation, followed by some on interpretation. Virtually every chapter will end with a question of application.

FULFILL YOUR ROLE

In summary, remember your role as a group leader. You are a

- discussion facilitator.
- tangent stopper.
- schedule maintainer.
- student encourager.
- Bible teacher (sometimes).

For additional help to fulfill your role, we recommend *Going Up: Lifting People to New Heights in Bible Study,* published by Churches Alive.

JESUS!
GOD IN YOU MADE POSSIBLE

JESUS!—CHAPTER 1
Immanuel

Luke 2:1-20

PERSPECTIVE: Luke, the writer of this gospel, was a physician and probably a Greek. He wrote his gospel with the Greeks in mind, presenting Jesus as the perfect man. Luke's care in collecting historical data about Jesus is evident, and his gospel is regarded as one of the best chronicles of Jesus' life. In Luke 2, you read about the perfect birth of the perfect man.

TEACHING OBJECTIVE: To show the humanity of Jesus.

DISCUSSION IDEAS:

2. Help the group members see the humanity of Jesus by asking, "What actions did you list that are common to most people?"

3. "Which of the descriptions emphasize the humanity of Jesus?"

   "Which ones emphasize that He is God with us?"

4. This question should stimulate group members to picture themselves at the scene. This will help them meditate on the passage and see the importance of the action (the angels' appearing).

5. Discussing this question should motivate group members to talk to others about Jesus. Be careful not to pressure people to do so. Allow them to grow at their individual rates.

6. Direct the discussion away from complaints about the commercial abuses of Christmas to talking about how to make it a Christ-honoring holiday.

Conclude your study by asking, "Why is it important that Jesus was totally human?" Possible answers include: to understand us, to communicate at our level, to be a perfect example, etc. Tell the group that next week they will focus on the divinity of Jesus.

SUMMARY: The birth of Jesus is a well-known story. Bethlehem, the star, and the manger are familiar to us. But many people miss the fact that Immanuel is God with us in Jesus Christ. He is man and He is divine.

The Word

John 1:1-18

PERSPECTIVE: John wrote this gospel that people "may believe that Jesus is the Christ" (John 20:31). He records fewer incidents from the life of Jesus than any of the other gospel writers, but each incident is developed more to encourage faith in Christ. John also presents Christ as the Son of God and emphasizes Jesus' divinity.

TEACHING OBJECTIVE: To show that Jesus is God in flesh. He is divine.

DISCUSSION IDEAS:

2. Use the clear statements of the passage to show that Jesus is the Word and that the Word is God. Emphasize to the group the need for starting with good observations about a passage before making interpretations of that passage.

3. Ask, "If Jesus were only a good religious leader, which of the benefits would we still have available to us?" This question leads to the importance of Jesus' divinity.

4. This question is one of several in the early chapters of this workbook that should help assure everyone of his or her salvation. If some people in the group are not clear about their relationship to God, take a few minutes to present the gospel, using John 1:12 as a beginning point.

5. Help the group members see the significance of what John said by asking, "What would you have thought if you were a Jew listening to John the Baptist?"

   "What did John say about Jesus that reinforces the fact that He is divine?"

6. Questions like this offer group members an opportunity to give their subjective responses to the content. By giving an opportunity to tell what the Scriptures mean to them,

group members are encouraged to explore the passage more deeply.

Conclude with a short discussion of the differences between the Christmas story in Luke and the Christmas story in John. Through this discussion you can unite the two emphases; Jesus was human, and He is divine.

SUMMARY: Jesus is the Word, and the Word is God. Jesus is fully God with us.

JESUS!—CHAPTER 3
Savior

John 3:1-21

PERSPECTIVE: As previously noted in chapter 2, John wrote this gospel to help people know and believe that Jesus is the Savior of the world. No doubt this is one of the primary reasons John chose to include this conversation with Nicodemus. Here is a religious leader coming to Jesus for answers to the basic questions of life.

TEACHING OBJECTIVE: To understand how to obtain salvation.

DISCUSSION IDEAS:

2. Rather than spending your time trying to analyze the abbreviated conversation, try to understand what both Nicodemus and Jesus were saying.

   "What do you think motivated Nicodemus to talk to Jesus about these issues?"

3. Be sure the group members begin by listing what the passage says about being born again. This is *observing*. Then ask what the passage means. This is *interpreting*. Because there are many confusing ideas about being born again, be sure those in the group make good observations *before* they express any interpretations.

4. Some people may have a difficult time understanding the story in Numbers 21 and relating it to Jesus as Savior. Be prepared to explain the story and how Jesus is like the bronze snake: It was a *type* of savior because it delivered the Israelites from the poison of real snakes.

5. These questions help to show that Jesus is the Savior. After quickly covering the questions, ask, "How does all this fit together in one complete idea?"

SUMMARY: Perhaps the best summary comes from another passage in the Bible, Hebrews 7:25: "Therefore he is able to save completely those who come to God through him, because he always lives to intercede for them."

JESUS!—CHAPTER 4

Friend of Sinners

John 4:4-26

PERSPECTIVE: John records a very unlikely conversation between a Jewish religious leader (Jesus) and a Samaritan woman. It violated many social taboos and customs. The woman in this conversation stands in sharp contrast with Nicodemus in the previous chapter. She is despised and considered by most Jews as no more important than a street dog. Yet Jesus talks with her, showing He is a friend to all sinners.

TEACHING OBJECTIVE: To show that Jesus wants to relate to you, no matter what you have done.

DISCUSSION IDEAS:
2. As group members give their versions of the conversation, encourage them by complimenting the good ideas they express.

3. Everyone should be able to identify in some ways with both Nicodemus and the woman. Look for similarities in motivation, social standing, emotions, past experiences, present circumstances, and so on.

4. The word *worship* is condensed from *worth-ship*. It is the act of acknowledging someone's worth. Ask the group, "How would you express the worth of God?" Then ask, "Why do you think we need to see the worth of God in spirit and in truth?"

6. Consider how your group could follow the example of Jesus. You might want to organize a group activity to communicate acceptance. This might be focused on neighbors, prisoners, or the homeless.

An appropriate way to conclude your meeting is to worshipfully sing, "What a Friend We Have in Jesus."

SUMMARY: Jesus is a friend to sinners. You may be rejected by others, scorned by religious people, and avoided by neighbors,

15

but He will welcome you as His friend. First, however, you must come to Him in *truth*, being honest about yourself and about who He is.

JESUS!—CHAPTER 5
Master

Matthew 8:23-9:8

PERSPECTIVE: Matthew wrote his gospel to show the Jews that Jesus was their promised Messiah. He often refers to Messianic prophecies that Jesus fulfilled. It is fitting that he describes the power of Jesus, for the Messiah must also be Master.

TEACHING OBJECTIVE: To show the mastery of Jesus over obstacles. He can be trusted in every area of life.

DISCUSSION IDEAS:

2. To show that Jesus is Master of all, ask, "What situation can you think of where the kind of authority demonstrated by Jesus is not sufficient?"

3. The demons illustrate the foolishness of not submitting to the authority of Jesus. Ask, "Why would you say the demons were foolish?"

   "What kind of people respond like these demons did?"

4. There are many possible answers to this question, so encourage a diversity of responses. One possible answer is that you can determine if a paralytic has been healed, but you can't be sure that he has been forgiven.

5. For the second part of this question, help the group members think about why people would respond each way. Point out that the best approach to each response is to attract people to Jesus. Don't "put people down" or show them how foolish they are.

6. Ask the group what evidence they can offer from their experiences that Jesus is Master today.

7. Expect different responses, including submitting to Jesus, trusting in Him, and looking for His will in all things.

SUMMARY: Jesus is Master—over all things. As Master, He is not in a position of having to plead for obedience. Just as the waves obey Him, all else will, too.

JESUS!—CHAPTER 6
Christ

Matthew 16:13-28

PERSPECTIVE: Matthew is the only gospel writer to include this episode, when Jesus clearly identifies Himself to His disciples. They had a difficult time understanding that their Christ would suffer; that was not their concept of the Messiah.

TEACHING OBJECTIVE: To show that Jesus clearly identified Himself as the Christ and foretold His crucifixion.

DISCUSSION IDEAS:

2. Don't try to discuss *all* the wrong ideas about Jesus—just some of the common ones. Examine a few of these to show why believing them can be dangerous.

3. "How are you like Peter in the first conversation and how are you like Peter in the second conversation?"

4. The Jews expected their Messiah (Christ) to live in triumph. They thought He would be their political and spiritual leader. Their expectations caused them to reject Jesus' comments about His coming death. To the contrary, we need to believe Jesus even when His words conflict with our logic and expectations.

5. Ask, "What can you do to 'die to self'?" Help move the discussion from general ideas to specific ones. For example, talking about giving up Monday night television to visit people at the hospital is more specific than saying you will deny yourself a favorite activity.

6. In biblical times, cities *defended* themselves with high walls and strong gates. Attacking armies usually would lay siege to a city and rush the gates (not the walls) when the people weakened. If the attackers won, it was said, "they overcame the gates." If the defenses held, it was said, "the gates overcame."

SUMMARY: Many people have wrong ideas about Jesus' identity. He is the Christ, the Son of the living God. He justified this claim by going to the Cross. If you are His follower, justify your claim by copying His example and dying to self.

JESUS!—CHAPTER 7
Servant

John 13:1-17

PERSPECTIVE: Almost half of John's Gospel describes the events beginning with the last week of Jesus' life. All four gospel writers tell about the Passover supper Jesus shared with His disciples, but only John records the account of Jesus serving them by washing their feet.

TEACHING OBJECTIVE: To show another side of Jesus, other than Master and Christ. He served and left us an example to serve others.

DISCUSSION IDEAS:

2. Help group members visualize the event by imagining some of the details not mentioned, such as the expressions on the disciples' faces, what they might have whispered to each other, and what they said to others later on.

3. If people are having a hard time answering the last question, you might share this insight: "Since Jesus was aware that He had all things under His power, He didn't need to flaunt it. Instead, He served. Many people today have a hard time serving because they are not sure of their position in God."

4. This question provides an opportunity for an application, perhaps involving the whole group. For example, volunteer to give the church kitchen a good cleaning.

5. Most of the titles show that Jesus should be served. Ask the group, "What titles do we have?" "Should we be served, or do the serving?"

6. Remember, when a question begins, "What do you consider," each person should record his individual conclusions and responses. Do not try to come to a consensus in the group.

This is a good opportunity to learn more about the people in your group. Their responses usually reflect their growth and needs.

SUMMARY: Jesus served His disciples by washing their feet, a job usually reserved for the servants. We should never consider ourselves too good to serve one another. There is no higher position than a servant.

JESUS!—CHAPTER 8
Bread of Life

Mark 14:12-42

PERSPECTIVE: Mark differs from John in many aspects. Instead of recording conversations, he records actions. He did this partly because he wished to present Jesus to the Romans, who were action-oriented. Mark tells us in concise language about the events surrounding the Last Supper, when Jesus presents Himself as the Bread of Life.

TEACHING OBJECTIVE: To understand the significance of the Last Supper and of Communion.

DISCUSSION IDEAS:

2. Help the group note the emphasis on action, not on detail and conversation. Point out this example of Mark's style as explained in the perspective information above.

4. Because there are differing ideas about Communion, it would be wise to talk to your pastor to gain his perspective. Perhaps he could give your group a brief explanation of the various opinions regarding Communion.

5. Jesus' comments reveal some of His thoughts. For example, calling God "Father" shows that He considered God to be close to Him. In saying, "Everything is possible for you," He acknowledged that God has unlimited power.

6. To find parallels to these actions, help the group look for the motivation behind each action. A betrayer, for example, has no loyalties or commitment. He is interested in the quick solution to a problem, not the right one.

7. Ask, "In what ways are you like the disciples?" "What lessons can you learn from their example?"

SUMMARY: When Jesus ate the Last Supper, He began one of the great observances for the Church. It is rich with meaning and tradition. When He went to pray in Gethsemane, He showed His torment and apprehension regarding the Cross.

Great High Priest
John 17

PERSPECTIVE: During Old Testament times, the high priest was the leading religious authority in Israel. He was consecrated, or set apart for that position, by special offerings and sacrifices. Though he also performed the same duties as other priests, once a year, on the Day of Atonement, he alone entered the Holy of Holies to mediate between God and the Israelites. The high priest was also the only one who could determine God's will on certain decisions. His word had absolute authority.

TEACHING OBJECTIVE: To understand Jesus' inner feelings and thoughts regarding His followers just prior to His death.

DISCUSSION IDEAS:

2. If people in the group ask why Jesus didn't pray for the world, ask them to draw their own conclusions.

3. "How should the fact that these things were uppermost in Jesus' mind affect your life on a daily basis?"

4. The questions emphasize that we glorify God by fulfilling His will.

5. Expect the group members to give responses similar to what is written in the passage. Encourage them to change biblical phrases like *not of the world* to more practical expressions such as *not concerned about prestige*. Explain that defining phrases as they complete their study will lead to greater understanding of the passage.

6. "What does Jesus say will happen when we practice oneness?"

7. Instead of having group members read their answers, spend time in prayer for the people listed.

SUMMARY: Jesus prayed for the glory of God and for the oneness of believers. We can participate in the fulfillment of His prayer. We glorify God when we are committed to obeying His will and living in unity.

Man of Sorrows

John 19:16-30

PERSPECTIVE: Hundreds of years before Jesus was born, Isaiah gave the coming Messiah the name Man of Sorrows (see Isaiah 53:3). Isaiah foretold that the Messiah would be so bruised and battered that He would be unrecognizable. But even this gruesome description fails to include Jesus' emotional anguish and spiritual torment on the Cross.

TEACHING OBJECTIVE: To appreciate the depth of God's love by seeing the degree of His sacrifice.

DISCUSSION IDEAS:
1. Some reference books may list a different order of events. Rather than discuss which is correct, attempt to visualize and empathize with the sufferings of Jesus.

2. This question gives people an opportunity to express their emotions as they consider what Jesus endured. Consider the emotional and spiritual pain as well as the physical agony.

3. Review how Peter did not understand the purpose of the Cross and began to argue with Jesus (studied in chapter 6). It is important to recognize that Jesus went to the Cross deliberately and willingly. It was not a defeat or a temporary setback. God was in control the whole time—not fate, not people, not the Devil.

4. You may wish to look at Hebrews 2:14-15 first because it relates to question 3 also. It is likely that the Devil thought he was gaining a victory by crucifying Jesus, but the Devil was the one who actually was being defeated.

   Use a concordance to demonstrate how to find verses about the Cross.

6. Discuss many ideas for the meaning of "It is finished" without debating the merits of each view. Share responses

to gain greater understanding of Jesus' statement and the study passage.

SUMMARY: Jesus died that we might live. This Man of Sorrows suffered immense pain that we might suffer none. His death was the darkest day of all history. That darkness would be overwhelming if we didn't know that it was part of God's plan, brought to a climax in Christ's glorious resurrection.

JESUS!—CHAPTER 11
Lord God Omnipotent
Luke 24

PERSPECTIVE: The depth of the darkness at the Crucifixion is a measure of the glory of the Resurrection. Jesus triumphed over death. Others have conquered illness or despair, but no one had defeated death—it won every battle until Jesus rose again. He gave the ultimate proof that He is Lord God Omnipotent.

TEACHING OBJECTIVES: To show that Jesus literally rose from the dead and to emphasize the significance of that triumph.

DISCUSSION IDEAS:
2. In addition to the evidence of His resurrection in the passage, encourage the group to offer other evidence, such as Jesus' prominence in all of history.

3. As you discuss the last part of question 3, point out that one person's faith may grow slower than another's. It is not important how rapidly you came to believe, but that you do believe.

4. This provides a good opportunity for encouraging individual application of Scripture. Suggest that each person in the group invite an unchurched person to his home. This doesn't complete your involvement in the commission Jesus gave, but it is a good first step. Ask, "How could having people in your home contribute to fulfilling Jesus' commission?"

5. Role play: Ask one of the well-prepared members of the group to defend Jesus' resurrection. You play the part of someone who considers His resurrection to be a hoax.

SUMMARY: Jesus rose from the dead. He conquered death completely. As Paul says, "Where, O death, is your victory? Where, O death, is your sting?" (1 Corinthians 15:55).

King of Kings
Acts 1:1-11

PERSPECTIVE: Jesus came to earth as part of a plan that preceded all creation. Abraham knew of it and rejoiced at the thought of seeing it (John 8:56).

Imagine the life of Jesus from Heaven's perspective. The Son of Glory has lived at His Father's right hand, with all things under His control. He leaves to enter human history to declare God to mortals and offer salvation to them. Now is the time of His return home to His throne—the King of kings is back. Think of the joy, the grandeur, the celebration.

TEACHING OBJECTIVE: To realize the fact and significance of the ascension of Jesus.

DISCUSSION IDEAS:
1. "How has it been helpful to you to read the study passage several times before answering the questions?"

2. Strangely enough, Scripture includes only these general comments about this period and a couple of specific events. Ask the group what they would have felt and done if they had heard about the Resurrection. It will help them visualize the events described in these cross-references.

3. It seems logical to assume that if Jesus remained on earth for 200 or 300 years after His resurrection, everyone would eventually hear about it and flock to see Him. Of course, those who would see Him would believe He rose, but would they be His followers? Perhaps they would only be satisfying their curiosity.

   One purpose of this question is to see that through His ascension, Jesus accomplished other things not recorded in the study passage.

4. Ask group members to tell what recent experiences they have had that qualify them to witness about Jesus.

28

6. "How does the Holy Spirit help us witness about Jesus Christ?"

SUMMARY: Since Jesus physically rose from the dead, He cannot die again. Today He reigns from a well-deserved throne in Heaven. He is King of kings.

ALIVE!
GOD IN INTIMATE
RELATIONSHIP WITH YOU

Giving New Life

2 Corinthians 5:11-21

PERSPECTIVE: Perhaps the harshest letters Paul wrote were to the Corinthian church. He addressed serious problems with blunt words of correction. The church was not demonstrating that they were different from the rest of the world. Fittingly, Paul wrote to them about expressing their new life in Christ through action that glorifies God.

TEACHING OBJECTIVE: To show that being alive in Christ means a new start affecting every area of your life.

DISCUSSION IDEAS:

1. This question offers an opportunity to give the quieter members of your group an opportunity to contribute to the discussion. As they tell what is meaningful to them, look for ways to carry those thoughts on to applications.

2. Often a dictionary will prove helpful even with well-known words. Encourage the group to use one often. You may also want to introduce the special advantages of a Bible dictionary at this time.

3. In the discussion, consider how these changed relationships affect your thoughts, feelings, actions, goals, motives, personality, etc.

4. It is easy to see the *fact* that we have exchanged our sinfulness for Christ's righteousness. But it is not always easy to apply this truth. Doing so, however, can help eliminate guilt feelings, depression, a sense of inferiority, and a host of other problems.

5. To emphasize the teaching of this verse, act out a situation in which a person is entering a foreign country and lists on the visa application the occupation of ambassador. The immigration authority asks questions such as, "What do you do as an ambassador?" "Where is your office?"

Afterward, ask how this role of an ambassador illustrates our roles as Christ's ambassadors.

Close your discussion by having some people read their journal entries from page 61. (For more information about the journal, see pages 5, 7 in *Alive!*)

SUMMARY: Being alive in Christ is a new start. All things begin fresh. You have a new relationship yielding intimate contact with God. You have new righteousness, a new job, a new title, and new responsibilities. All of these gifts should result in new actions and attitudes.

ALIVE!—CHAPTER 2
Lighting Your Way

1 John 1:1-10

PERSPECTIVE: John the Apostle wrote both the Gospel of John and 1 John. In both, he presents God as light near the beginning (John 1:4-9 and 1 John 1:5-7). In the Gospel, he says that the light is life and that John the Baptist came to testify to the light so all could believe. In this epistle, he talks of *continuing* in the light as part of deepening your intimacy with God.

TEACHING OBJECTIVE: To show that light enables you to be honest about yourself, which results in fellowship with God.

DISCUSSION IDEAS:
1. Use this question to reinforce what the group learned about defining words last week.

   In verse 7, the word *we* in the phrase *we have fellowship* could refer to you and God or you and other believers. Each view leads to valid applications for life.

2. "Is it what we say with our mouths or our hearts that matters?"

5. Other questions that may help develop these ideas:

   "What does it indicate about you if you have better relationships with those who are in darkness than those who are in the light?"

   "If you can't fellowship with those in darkness, how can you relate to them?"

   "If a Christian is walking in darkness, with whom do you think he can have fellowship?"

Conclude your discussion time by asking several people to read their journal entries for chapter 2.

SUMMARY: Walking in the light is part of being alive and in intimate contact with God because it enables you to maintain fellowship with Him. He allows this fellowship to continue as long as you honestly admit your sins.

Residing in You

Romans 8:5-17

PERSPECTIVE: When you became alive in Christ, God established such intimate contact with you that He actually took up residence *in* you. This residence is not merely for convenience; it is to take control. One might say that the more God is in control of you, the more you are alive in Him.

TEACHING OBJECTIVE: To be assured of the indwelling of the Holy Spirit.

DISCUSSION IDEAS:
1. You can use this question to help group members increase their Bible study skills by recognizing and analyzing contrasts. You may also wish to note comparisons.

2. It is important that the group members recognize *their* nature as opposite to the Holy Spirit's nature. Many people think of the difference as slight or moderate, but not opposite. Seeing this sharp contrast can motivate people to allow the Spirit to control them.

3. "Are these statements true of you even when you don't feel they are?" "What should you do in that case?"

4. Use this opportunity to eliminate anxiety about walking in the Spirit. We do not have to wonder if God is willing to walk with us, but only if we are willing to walk with Him.

5. Help those in the group apply the truths they express. For example, if someone says that thinking about Scripture helps, encourage him to formulate a plan to memorize some verses so he *can* think about them.

6. Lead the discussion toward positive steps such as meditating on Scripture, talking to the pastor or church leader, and reading more about the Holy Spirit.

Conclude your discussion time by asking several people to share their journal entries with the group.

SUMMARY: Being alive in Christ includes His indwelling—the most intimate contact. Your flesh rebels at this notion and is opposed to God's control. Nevertheless, the Christ-controlled life is both your privilege and obligation.

ALIVE!—CHAPTER 4
Providing Fullness

Colossians 2:6-17

PERSPECTIVE: Many of the people living in Colosse were being confused by men who taught that a person must do more than simply receive Christ to be acceptable to God. One purpose of the Apostle Paul, who wrote this letter to that church, was to show that being alive in Christ and in intimate contact with God means having the fullness of God. They didn't need anything else.

TEACHING OBJECTIVE: To recognize our completeness in Jesus so we do not look for additional spiritual experiences to gain salvation.

DISCUSSION IDEAS:
1. If some group members have newborns, have them describe their babies' completeness to enhance the illustration. Ask about the babies' growth and look for parallels to spiritual growth.

2. Many new Christians have had the experience of going from spiritual fulfillment to spiritual frustration later on. To remain fulfilled, we must maintain the same attitudes, faith, and dependence on God as when we received Christ.

3. "What difference does it make if you fail to believe that you are complete?"

4. Help your group go beyond the information in the verses to draw further conclusions. For example, in verse 6, Jesus is presented as the source of salvation and the means to maturity.

5. Ask, "Why is it necessary to take things away to provide fullness?" (Refinishing furniture is a good illustration. The old varnish must be removed in order to put a good finish on it.)

Conclude your discussion time by asking several people to share their journal entries for chapter 4.

SUMMARY: We receive Christ by faith, through His grace, offering none of our own righteousness, and we must continue to walk in Him in the same way. Since we are complete in Him, we need nothing else. As complete as Christ is, so are we.

Granting You Access
Hebrews 4:12-16

PERSPECTIVE: To the Jews, God was very sacred, but also very remote. He resided in the Holy of Holies in the Temple. Only one man, the high priest, could enter that sacred place—and then, only once a year. In Hebrews, the writer explains our more intimate and frequent contact with God through our High Priest, Jesus Christ. We have full access to God.

TEACHING OBJECTIVE: To understand that God welcomes your presence; it is not an interruption, nor an imposition.

DISCUSSION IDEAS:
Begin your discussion by asking several people to share their journal entries with the group.

1. Have several people read their main thoughts from verses 12 through 16. Don't have several people read their thoughts from 12, then several from 13, etc. It disrupts the flow.

2. Review the background information to help the group think like Jews in Old Testament times. Keeping their religious background in mind will help the group understand what the Jewish Christians thought when Hebrews was written.

3. Many people feel guilty when they are tempted. Since Christ was tempted, we must conclude there is nothing wrong with temptation. Properly handled, temptation can help you draw close to God.

5. We should not feel bad about ourselves when we are tempted. We are still in intimate contact with God, and He lights our way. Ask, "What did you learn in 1 John 1 that relates to this subject?"

6. Point out that Jesus is the perfect friend.

SUMMARY: Your intimate contact with God need not be threatened by your temptations. He will supply grace for you to succeed in overcoming temptation, and have mercy on you if you fail. He understands your predicament because your High Priest has been tempted, too.

ALIVE!—CHAPTER 6
Giving You Guidance

John 16:5-15

PERSPECTIVE: These words of Jesus were spoken during the week prior to His death. Here He tells how His relationship with the disciples will change, but without losing its intimacy. He will give guidance through the Holy Spirit.

TEACHING OBJECTIVE: To know that the Holy Spirit provides daily guidance.

DISCUSSION IDEAS:

1. This exercise is similar to others in which the group members listed one action for each verse in a passage. Again, the purpose is to see the overall flow. Some people may try too hard to determine which of several concepts in a verse is *the* main one. For example, there are at least three possibilities for the main thought of verse 7: "I tell you the truth"; "I'm leaving for your good"; and "I will send the Counselor." Reading the context should help select one. But if group members indicate they are bogged down deciding between main thoughts, encourage them to just choose one and move along.

2. "What are other names He has?" "What do they imply?"

3. This question can be answered by a short phrase from the indicated verses; for example, "He will convict the world." Discuss what this means and how it applies to those in the group. Encourage them to go beyond simple, obvious answers.

4. Be sure your group discusses two sides of the issue; the Holy Spirit's convicting power will encourage you to talk at times and *not* talk at other times. Ask, "Knowing that the Holy Spirit is convicting the world, when should you initiate a conversation about Jesus, and when should you be silent?"

6. Ask group members to tell how the Holy Spirit has guided them.

In chapter 3 of this guide, the group studied the indwelling of the Holy Spirit and His control. Ask, "What is the difference between the Spirit's guidance and His control?"

Remember to have several people share their journal entries.

SUMMARY: Jesus wanted to be with all of His disciples at the same time. Since He could not do this in His physical body, He returned to Heaven and sent the Holy Spirit to each of us. He is your Counselor, Comforter, and Guide. He guides you in and through truth, which is the Word of God (John 17:17). His guidance is for your good, the world's conviction, and Jesus' glory.

ALIVE!—CHAPTER 7
Being Your Companion
Psalm 27

PERSPECTIVE: Although the Psalms are part of the Old Testament, they still express many thoughts and feelings that apply today. David, the writer of this psalm, was known as a "man after God's heart." He expresses the warmth and intimacy of a person who enjoys God's companionship.

TEACHING OBJECTIVE: To create a desire for companionship with God that leads to specific action.

DISCUSSION IDEAS:

1. Ask, "What do you know about David?" to establish the background for studying Psalm 27.

   Follow with, "How are we like David?" which should lead to seeing that the benefits David listed in the psalm apply to us, also.

3. A promise is any statement made by God that tells what He will do for you. You can often find a promise on a specific subject by using a concordance.

   Instead of using a lot of time discussing the requests, submit them to God.

4. In verse 4, David refers to "the house of the Lord." In other verses he also mentions the temple and the tabernacle. Point out that these structures do not exist today. Ask, "What has taken their place?" and turn to 1 Corinthians 3:16-17.

5. "What things cause your confidence in God to grow?"

   "How does your confidence affect the way you live?"

6. Fear is a great crippler. It inhibits many positive actions. Help the group deal with common fears such as failure, rejection, intimacy, and witnessing.

7. "When have you had to wait for the Lord?"

8. Each person should have one specific project to do for this exercise.

Ask several people to read their journal entries aloud.

SUMMARY: Enjoying God's companionship is part of His plan for you. It takes right attitudes and action on your part. The benefits reach every area of life.

ALIVE!—CHAPTER 8
Assuring Your Triumph

Romans 8:28-39

PERSPECTIVE: Paul was well qualified to write about confidence of triumph. He endured prison, beatings, floggings, exposure, stonings, persecution, hunger, fatigue, betrayal, shipwrecks, and more (see 2 Corinthians 11:23-28). Still, he was sure of God's love and his triumph. He could see God's sovereign hand despite all these hardships.

TEACHING OBJECTIVE: To know that you are triumphing regardless of your circumstances.

DISCUSSION IDEAS:

1. Ask, "What is the good toward which all things contribute?" If your group has difficulty answering, point them to verse 29.

3. The context of verse 28 indicates that the phrase *all things* refers to our circumstances. In verse 32, *all things* cannot refer to physical items, for not everyone has riches or many things. Thinking along this line will help you define *all things*.

4. Carefully studying verse 36 and the context will show that conquering does *not* necessarily mean alleviating hard times, but does mean going through them victoriously. Hebrews 11:32-38 contains a list of people who conquered, some by alleviation and some by endurance.

5. Help your group members see that most of their fears are based upon *this world's* views. Give the examples of the world's thinking that are listed below and ask the group for a true perspective of each one.

   Money brings security.
   Clothes make the man.
   Growing old is a curse.
   Death is tragic.

46

6. Give an example of how God enabled you to triumph in some circumstance by claiming a promise. Then ask the group for examples from their lives.

Remember to include time for members to share their journal entries.

SUMMARY: God weaves together your experiences to make you Christlike. None of these experiences separate you from God or are caused by His displeasure. No matter what your hardships, you are more than a conqueror.

ALIVE!—CHAPTER 9
Reviving by His Word
Psalm 19:7-11

PERSPECTIVE: Verses 1-6 of Psalm 19, although not included in the study passage, give a foundation for it by presenting some knowledge of God through natural revelation (that which can be learned about God from observing nature). In nature, we can see the hand of an intelligent Creator. He is orderly, universal, and has capacity beyond understanding. In the study passage (verses 7-11), the psalmist presents the direct revelation of God by His Word. Natural revelation gives a general knowledge of God, but His Word revives your very soul.

TEACHING OBJECTIVE: To realize that refreshment is available in God's Word.

DISCUSSION IDEAS:
Begin your discussion by having several people share their journal entries.

1. Ask the group to describe each benefit in different words.

2. This is an exercise in visualization. By visualizing what may have happened to David, you can often understand his motives and feelings.

3. To help everyone make applications, ask, "How does the verse you chose help you today?"

4. If someone in the group has another way to spend time in the Word, let him explain it. Use the exercise to encourage new ideas, not limit them.

5. Ask, "Why are there some Christians who do not gain these rewards?" Help your group see their responsibility to feed on God's Word to get the desired results.

6. This exercise helps group members taste the Word, and hopefully will increase their appetites for it.

SUMMARY: God's Word is for your advantage. It revives you, teaches you, strengthens you, and guides you through life. It is not a rule book that limits your options, but the truth that leads to your fulfillment.

ALIVE!—CHAPTER 10
Responding to Your Prayers
Matthew 6:5-15

PERSPECTIVE: The Lord's Prayer, as the study passage is commonly called, is usually quoted from Matthew 6. The parallel passage in Luke 11 tells that Jesus taught this prayer in response to a request from the disciples. They had listened to Him praying, and asked to be taught to pray.

Introduce the study by saying, "People usually don't feel any need to be taught how to talk to others. Why do they often feel a need to be taught how to talk to God?"

TEACHING OBJECTIVE: To learn to use this model prayer.

DISCUSSION IDEAS:
1. "How do some people do these things today?"

2. This question relates prayer to your intimate relationship with God. Ask, "Does what is revealed about God make you feel closer to Him or more distant?"

3. After some discussion on these elements of prayer, spend about twelve minutes in prayer. Ask group members to bow their heads and take turns reading their prayers out loud. Lead the group through this by saying, "Let's take two minutes to worship God in prayer" ("Hallowed be your name"). Then, two minutes later, move on to the next element, and so on through the remainder of the prayer.

4. Don't try to answer the question of how these statements relate to salvation by grace. Focus on the application: we need to be forgiving.

Close your time in group prayer, using journal entries as a basis for thanking God for what He has done and requesting help to fulfill individual responsibilities.

SUMMARY: Jesus left us a model that balances prayer, focused on God, on others, and on ourselves. Though we need not quote these words in every prayer, we should, in general, maintain the same focuses and balance.

Meriting Your Trust

Psalm 37:1-11

PERSPECTIVE: You receive maximum benefit from prayer and feeding on God's Word (chapters 9 and 10) when you have the right attitudes. One of the attitudes that causes these activities to enhance your spiritual well-being is a confident trust in God.

TEACHING OBJECTIVE: To understand that God is worthy of your trust.

DISCUSSION IDEAS:
1. "How do God's commands increase your enjoyment of life?"

2. "If a person doesn't trust you, how does it affect your attitude toward him or her?"

   "If a person doesn't trust God, do you think it affects God's attitude the same way?"

3. "Why can we say that not leaning on your understanding does not mean putting your brain on hold?"

4. If members of the group are having a tough time thinking of personal experiences, approach it from the negative. For example, ask, "Why don't you delight in some people?" "Who do you delight in? Why?"

5. The person who envies the wicked does not see the whole picture. Ask, "What did the wicked have to give up to get the benefits they enjoy?" "Is their prosperity worth it?"

Remember to include time for people to share their journal entries.

SUMMARY: God is worthy of your trust. It will enhance your relationship to Him and yield positive benefits for your life. Don't envy the wicked when they prosper. There will ultimately come a time in their lives when they would rather have the peace and comfort God gives you than their "prosperity."

51

Sustaining Your Life

John 15:1-17

PERSPECTIVE: During His last week on earth, Jesus gave this instruction about the intimate contact He wants to have with His followers. One reason this passage concludes this study book is that it summarizes many of the thoughts found in other chapters.

TEACHING OBJECTIVE: To maintain a close relationship with God by remaining in and being sustained by Jesus Christ.

DISCUSSION IDEAS:
1. Have one person read his key words for the passage. Then ask the group if it enabled them to recall the thrust of the passage. The purpose is to see how a few words can help people recall major concepts.

2. This is a good passage for which to use a variety of translations. Seeing how other versions interpret the word *remain* will give you a clearer understanding of what is being taught.

3. Point out that analogies are used to simplify a concept, but they usually break down at some point. Ask, "What are some ways we are not like vines?"

4. "What kind of fruit do we bear?"

6. Review the chapter titles in *Alive!* to see how many of those concepts are included in this passage. This helps tie the book together.

Have those in the group compare this study passage to their journals to help summarize what they learned in this book.

SUMMARY: Jesus expects you to remain in Him. Just as a branch is no longer part of the vine and dies when cut off, you are incapable of life apart from Christ. When you remain in Him,

He will treat you just like any master gardener would treat his plants. He'll make you grow, flourish, reproduce, and be healthy in every way.

RICH!
GOD MEETING
YOUR DEEPEST NEEDS

RICH!—CHAPTER 1
Love

1 John 4:7-21

PERSPECTIVE: This book begins with love because it is the foundation of your other riches. Everyone has a deep need to be loved. God meets this need by loving you with a love that depends only on His character, not on your loveliness.

TEACHING OBJECTIVE: To know that God loves you and will empower you to love others.

DISCUSSION IDEAS:
1. Ask, "How is love described in songs today?" "Are these good descriptions of love?" "Why or why not?" This will open discussion about God's love and how to describe it.

2. Some possible answers:

   "When bad things happen, I rely on God's love to cause them to turn out all right."

   "When I need guidance, I remind myself that His guidance is motivated by love."

   "When I sin, I rely on His love to forgive me."

3. One purpose of this question is to see that we should love others not because they deserve it, but because God loves them.

4. "What does it mean if you feel love toward others but don't translate it into action?"

5. "Is there any difference between loving your spouse and loving others?"

SUMMARY: The flow of love can be followed. It begins with God. He is the Fountainhead. It flowed from Him to us through Christ on the Cross, the greatest act of love. Having flowed into us, it should continue moving on to others.

RICH!—CHAPTER 2
Grace

Ephesians 2:1-10

PERSPECTIVE: God's love motivates His grace, the unmerited favor He shows toward us. We cannot earn anything. We are not placed on a scale of balances to see what we deserve. By grace, God chooses to bestow great riches, benefits, and advantages on us.

TEACHING OBJECTIVE: To show the total sufficiency of God's grace.

DISCUSSION IDEAS:
1. To explore the concept of grace, ask the group to give some illustrations of grace on a human level. For example, "Because of illness and late assignments, I should have failed my philosophy course in college, but the prof chose to give me a passing grade."

2,3. Many people don't feel they are as bad as verses 2 and 3 present. But seeing God's perspective of your past and present will help you understand the extent of His grace.

4. This question allows you to help those in the group keep a balanced view about the subject of good works and grace. There are two wrong conclusions people have made. Examine them by asking, "What's wrong with the idea that you can do enough good deeds to get into Heaven?" "What's wrong with thinking that salvation by grace means it doesn't matter if you do any good deeds?"

6. The following verses can help people gain confidence in God's grace:

   Romans 5:20-21
   Romans 8:32
   Romans 11:6
   2 Thessalonians 2:16-17

2 Timothy 1:8-10
1 John 5:14-15

SUMMARY: God saw that your life at one time was a despicable and horrid sight. To Him, it was without redeeming value. By grace, He transformed you into the likeness of His Son — with His righteousness. You didn't earn it. Your good works didn't merit it. But now that you are saved, good works should characterize your life.

RICH!—CHAPTER 3
Peace

Philippians 4:1-9

PERSPECTIVE: God's love and grace would be of limited value to us if we had to live with constant inner turmoil. They would be frozen assets—not usable riches. Because trials are good for us, God's love does not remove them. But His grace will take us through them with His peace.

TEACHING OBJECTIVE: To know how to gain God's peace in the midst of trials.

DISCUSSION IDEAS:
1. Stress the relationship between obedience to God's commands and the peace that follows. This shows that God's commands are not difficult requisites for gaining His favor, but practical steps you can take to gain what you desire—peace.

2. "Can anyone give an illustration of obeying these commands?" "What resulted?"

3. Ask, "When is tension between people productive, and when is it destructive?" The purpose is to show that tension by itself is not harmful. Wrong attitudes cause tension to become destructive.

5. You can use this exercise to show that there are always reasons to thank God.

   Ask, "What should you do if you don't feel grateful?" This question will introduce the idea that we can thank God regardless of our emotional state.

SUMMARY: Peace from God is not always understandable, but it is obtainable. Focus your attention on God and rejoice in Him, not your circumstances. Gentleness will reduce tension with others. Above all, don't worry. Pray! Be grateful for all God has done, and His peace will surround you. Practice thankful thinking, focusing on all that is good, true, and beautiful.

RICH!—CHAPTER 4
Acceptance
Luke 5:11-32

PERSPECTIVE: Most of us are familiar with the story of the prodigal son. It is more than a tale of a rebellious teenager who returns home. It reveals the attitude of God toward us. His willingness to accept us no matter how vile we've acted is an important part of our riches because most of us have acted in rebellion toward God at some time.

TEACHING OBJECTIVE: To know that God is always willing to receive you back into His good graces.

DISCUSSION IDEAS:
1. "In what ways have you been like the prodigal son?"

2. "In giving the boy his inheritance, how is the father like our heavenly Father?"

3. "What would be some present-day parallels to asking for your portion, living it up, and feeding pigs?"

4. People often express the idea that the Christian life is an ordeal, lacking fun and enjoyment. In fact, it is *for* our enjoyment. The reasonable and sensible thing is to walk with God.

5. "What characteristics of God was Jesus trying to teach His followers?"

6. Some people who have lived wholesome lives cannot readily identify with the prodigal son. This question can help these people apply this story to themselves.

7. This is *not* a trivial question. Proverbs 29:1 seems to bring out a different point than the parable teaches. Because there are varieties of responses, it would be good to discuss this with your pastor to gain his perspective and insight.

SUMMARY: Being rebellious and leaving the shelter of your Father's care may seem like fun, but it brings bitter results. The sensible response is to return to Him. Though you are unworthy, He celebrates your return.

Clear Conscience

Hebrews 10:1-14

PERSPECTIVE: Parts of Hebrews are very difficult to understand because the book was written for Jews who had left the old covenant to follow Jesus. A main theme in the Book of Hebrews is that our riches in Christ are far superior to any advantages under the old covenant. One superior benefit is a *cleared* conscience instead of covered guilt.

TEACHING OBJECTIVE: To know that we need not allow guilt to rule our lives.

DISCUSSION IDEAS:

1. Discuss responses relatively quickly. The underlining is largely an exercise of preparation for answering other questions.

2. "What difference between living under the law and living in Christ impressed you most?"

3. Some possible answers: "Shadows are two-dimensional, while objects are three-dimensional." "The object determines the shape of the shadow."

4. Some members of the group may argue that sometimes this attempt does work. If they do, don't disagree with them. Instead, ask, "Does it work in the same sense that Christ clears our conscience?"

    Romans 3:27-28 and Galatians 2:16-20 help answer the second part of the question.

6. Help the group members leave the group with a clear conscience by applying what is learned in this exercise.

SUMMARY: In the old system (before Christ), a once-a-year sacrifice paid the penalty for sins. Now, a once-for-all-time sacrifice (Christ's death) has removed them so we can have a clear conscience. This new system is so superior to the old that it completely replaces it.

Wisdom
Proverbs 2

PERSPECTIVE: Israel was a united nation under only three kings: Saul ruled from 1050 to 1010 BC; David from 1010 to 973 BC; and Solomon from 973 to 933 BC. Solomon's reign was characterized by peace and prosperity. He also built the Temple during his rule. This edifice was one of the largest and most ornate in all of history. But despite his great accomplishments, Solomon was led astray by his 700 wives and 300 concubines — who introduced him to other gods.

TEACHING OBJECTIVE: To show that God's wisdom is superior to worldly wisdom.

DISCUSSION IDEAS:
1. Discuss question 1 at the same time you discuss question 7.

2. "What attitudes are indicated in these verses?"

3. "Verses 6-11 refer to being shielded, guarded, and protected (twice). In what ways do you believe wisdom protects your life?"

4. "What do these wicked men look like today?"

    "Where might you run into these adulterous women?"

6. In your discussion, you'll need to decide what the word *best* means.

7. Have the people in your group give short and spontaneous answers to the following questions. Allow no more than one minute per question. Afterward, discuss the qualities of a wise person.

    What kind of career does a wise person have?

    What kind of hobbies?

    What kind of education?

Does the wise person have a crowded schedule?

What kind of books does a wise person read?

What kind of clothes does a wise person wear?

SUMMARY: Wisdom protects you from many problems and enables you to live morally and justly. It will also deliver you from those who would deceive you with perverse ideas and practices. Wisdom comes from God, and it must be pursued diligently.

Comfort

2 Corinthians 1:3-11

PERSPECTIVE: Paul's first letter to Corinth included several sharp rebukes. He told them that they were spiritual babies (1 Corinthians 3:1), that they should deal harshly with an open case of adultery (1 Corinthians 5), and that their communion services were disgraceful (1 Corinthians 11:20-22). Evidently they corrected many of these wrongs, and Paul changed his tone in the second letter to comfort. He told them to forgive and comfort the repentant adulterer (2 Corinthians 2:7), and said that he took great joy in them (2 Corinthians 7:4).

TEACHING OBJECTIVE: To know how to appropriate God's comfort.

DISCUSSION IDEAS:

1. To show the importance of growing through trials, ask, "Why doesn't God comfort us by simply removing our problems?"

2. "What are other names for God that reveal His desire to comfort you?"

3. "What other purposes can there be for God to comfort you?"

4. Help the group members realize that their emotions are wrong only when they cause wrong behavior. We should acknowledge the feelings we have so we can keep them from overwhelming us.

5. The passage presents a balanced approach: Paul worked toward gaining comfort; others prayed for it; and God granted it. Comfort may not come to those who sit back and wait for it.

   "What can you do to help find comfort?"

   "Whose comfort should we pray for?"

65

"What can we as a church do to comfort others?"

7. Anticipate that some people may honestly feel both ways.

SUMMARY: God is a compassionate Comforter. He cares, and will comfort you, sometimes by the prayers of others, other times by a visit from a friend, or at times, by deliverance. Your comfort is more than a blessing; it is equipping you to help and comfort others.

Freedom

Galatians 5:1-18

PERSPECTIVE: Paul wrote the letter to the church at Galatia because false teachers had convinced many Christians that they had to add certain actions to the work of Christ to be pleasing to God. Paul asserted that through faith in Christ alone we are saved *and* live. We are not under bondage to circumcision or sacrifices or anything else in order to please God. In Christ we are free from these obligations.

TEACHING OBJECTIVE: To live in the freedom of Christ without perverting it to license.

DISCUSSION IDEAS:
1. "What are other aspects of slavery and freedom not mentioned in this passage?"

2. Be careful not to spend too much time discussing this question. Though interesting, long discussion will keep you from other important teachings in this passage.

3. Anything other than faith is a form of bondage because if it is necessary, it must be obeyed. If obeyed, it is your master and you are its slave. We are Christ's slaves, but free from all other bondage.

4. Verse 2 must be interpreted in light of the context of the passage. Even today, many males are circumcized as infants, but they are not automatically estranged from Christ. Christ is of no value to those who practice circumcision (or any other act) for the purpose of establishing their own righteousness. We must totally depend upon His righteousness, not ours.

5. To show the freedom that comes from obeying the truth, ask, "What happens when we follow a lie?"

7. Although there are many ideas about how to live by the Spirit, the following simple plan has helped many:

Confess any known sin (1 John 1:9).

Ask God to fill you with His Spirit (Ephesians 5:18).

Believe that you are filled according to His promise (1 John 5:14-15).

SUMMARY: Christ has set us free. It is wrong and foolish to encumber ourselves with binding obligations. Either these regulations are of value or Christ is of value, not both. The truth we should obey is that we are justified by faith in Christ. Then, in freedom, we act in love to serve others as we live by His Spirit.

Provision

Matthew 6:19-34

PERSPECTIVE: Imagine a society without social security, welfare, retirement plans, insurance, medicare, food stamps, or even a soup line. It is easy to see why many people during New Testament times were concerned about the necessities of life. Though society today provides many of those safeguards, you cannot ultimately trust them.

TEACHING OBJECTIVE: To know and rely on God's provision, rather than worrying about the future.

DISCUSSION IDEA:
1. To bring out that Jesus is interested in our benefit, not in restricting our actions, ask, "What do you think motivated Jesus to give these commands?"

2. When possible, amplify the question Jesus asked to include other possibilities; for example, "Is life more important than money or fun or happiness?"

3. Some people may not like thinking of God as Father because they have a bad image of fathers. Ask, "What would help people who have a bad father image gain a better understanding of the nature of God?"

5. Help the group talk about the actual concerns that they have. They need to expect His provision by faith.

7. "How does our church help you seek righteousness?"

8. "What would you suggest that Bill do?"

SUMMARY: God has always taken care of His creatures. Birds have food. Hills are crowned with beautiful robes of flowers. Since you are more precious than these things, you can expect God to provide for you, too. With this worry eliminated, you can concentrate on your major quest—God's Kingdom and His righteousness.

RICH!—CHAPTER 10
Family

Acts 2:41-47

PERSPECTIVE: Acts is primarily a history book. It has little in the way of directives, correctives, and doctrine. It is full of examples, some to be followed, some to be avoided. The Jerusalem church provides a positive example of what God intends for your life—a caring family.

TEACHING OBJECTIVE: To enjoy the benefits of your local church.

DISCUSSION IDEAS:

1. "How would you like it if suddenly we had 3,000 new members at church?" "What problems would we have?"

   "Why do many people really prefer keeping a church small?"

2. "How is love demonstrated in our church?" "How can we improve our ministry of love?"

4. If you investigate, you will probably find some people in your church who need help with food and/or clothing. As part of the discussion of this question, develop a plan for a group project to help others.

6. "If you were to join the Jerusalem church described in these verses, would you fit in? Why or why not?"

7. Be sure to keep your discussion positive. Talk about good aspects of your church and suggestions that you can act on. Don't get off into criticism or improvement suggestions that are beyond your influence.

SUMMARY: The early Church set a challenging example. People cared so much for one another that they sacrificed their possessions for the good of others. They grew spiritually through good doctrine and prayer. They developed socially by becoming good friends and meeting in small groups. These relationships were not exclusive; believers worked to include more and more people.

Courage

Matthew 14:22-33

PERSPECTIVE: Although several of the disciples were former fishermen, they all had good reason to be afraid of storms on the Sea of Galilee. Because it is surrounded by mountains, it is prone to sudden and violent storms. Cold mountain air accelerates down the slopes toward the sea, sometimes from all sides at once. The pressure on the water and the high winds from more than one direction create a force that can tear a boat apart in minutes. These storms arise so quickly that even during a calm sea fishermen are alert. At times the sea has gone from calmness to storm in less than ten minutes, truly a situation for daring courage.

TEACHING OBJECTIVE: To be able to appropriate God's courage to overcome fears.

DISCUSSION IDEAS:

1. Have a few people read their complete lists of statements to get an overview of the action. Then ask, "Other than fear and courage, what emotions do you think the disciples felt?"

2. Anticipate that members of the group will answer both ways. The question helps them place themselves in the story to gain insight.

3. Help the group see that they often go through the same process as Peter when fears overcome them. Move the discussion from what Peter should have done to what they should do.

4. This question illustrates the fact that firm convictions can give you courage. Ask, "How do we gain convictions like those the disciples had?"

6. "What do you plan to do?"

SUMMARY: Everyone faces frightening situations that require courage. Peter illustrates our plight; he demonstrated both courage (as he got out of the boat) and fear (as he began to sink). Jesus wants to give us courage to get out of our "boat." If we find ourselves sinking, He is quick to rescue us.

RICH!—CHAPTER 12
Hope

1 Thessalonians 4:13-5:11

PERSPECTIVE: Some false teachers came to the church at Thessalonica, saying that only those who were on earth during the return of Jesus would go with Him to Heaven. In his letter to the Thessalonians, Paul included considerable instruction about the Lord's return to correct this and other false ideas and give the people a prevailing hope.

TEACHING OBJECTIVE: To know that Jesus' return is our hope.

DISCUSSION IDEAS:
1. "What future certainty encourages you the most? Why?"

2. Since there are so many schools of thought regarding the order and timing of the events surrounding the return of Christ, expect a diversity of ideas. Talk to your pastor about his understanding to prepare for this discussion. Avoid dogmatism on this subject; list the things that will happen without trying to get them in a "correct" sequence. Don't allow this interaction to consume your entire discussion time.

3. "What would be another way to end this sentence: 'The return of Christ is like . . .'?"

5. These are applications of the doctrine of the return of Christ, but not the only applications. To discuss other possibilities, ask, "How should having the hope of Christ's return affect us on a day-to-day basis?"

6. Use the lists of riches as a summary of this book. Compare the lists with the table of contents of this book to find similarities.

SUMMARY: Jesus will return, lifting all Christians to Heaven with Him, whether dead or alive. It will happen suddenly but not unexpectedly. People in darkness are ignorant of this certainty and live riotiously. People in the light live righteously, encouraging one another until our hope is realized.

POWERFUL!
GOD ENABLING YOU

POWERFUL!—CHAPTER 1
Over Adversaries

1 Kings 18:16-40

PERSPECTIVE: Elijah the prophet spoke the words of God to Israel during the first half of the ninth century BC. This was approximately 100 years after the nation of Israel split into two kingdoms. His most notable deeds are his prayer for rain to be withheld for 3½ years and the defeat of Baal's prophets.

TEACHING OBJECTIVE: To show that God's power is available when we face seemingly overwhelming odds.

DISCUSSION IDEAS:

1. This exercise helps group members review the event and relate the story to today, realizing it is not a super-hero fairy tale. Ask, "Could something like this happen today? How?"

4. Some verses that have helped others make decisions:

   1 Corinthians 6:12—Does it benefit all concerned?

   1 Corinthians 10:31—Does it glorify God?

   Colossians 3:2—Does it focus on things above?

5. Ask for examples of people using God's power to overcome obstacles.

6. Ask, "Do you think knowing the right words to pray is the key to power? If not, what is the key?"

SUMMARY: It is unlikely that anyone today will encounter a situation similar to Elijah's. Yet, we have parallel experiences. Elijah felt lonely (see 1 Kings 19:10). He faced overwhelming odds (500 to 1). He was in an impossible situation. Like Elijah, we need God's power to overcome our adversaries.

By the Scriptures
2 Timothy 3:14-4:5

PERSPECTIVE: As far as we can tell, the Jews have accepted the books of the Old Testament as Scripture from the times of their origin. Through the years, there have been numerous reorganizations without changing the content. For example, all the minor prophets (Hosea through Malachi) were once considered one book.

The New Testament, of course, was not formed when Paul wrote this epistle to Timothy. But the words of Jesus were evidently considered Scripture by the apostles. Twenty-seven books were formally adopted as the New Testament in AD 397 by the church fathers at the Council of Carthage.

TEACHING OBJECTIVE: To show the power of the Scriptures to help a person live a better life.

DISCUSSION IDEAS:
1. It is likely your group will compile an impressive list of facts about the Scriptures. Relate God's Word to life by asking, "How can what we know about the Bible help us in daily situations?"

2. To ensure that you have adequate information about the inspiration of Scripture, talk to your pastor in advance of your group meeting.

3. "How do you determine when a situation needs rebuke and/or correction?"

   Because these are done so seldom, help the group see the benefits of rebuke and correction by asking, "Why should we consider rebuke something done *for* us instead of *to* us?"

6. Help the group see that a person's response should not determine how and when we use the Scriptures. Also, see Isaiah 55:10-11.

7. Note that the first reference is primarily useful toward

using the Word with others, and the last reference is useful for yourself.

SUMMARY: The Bible is our authority for belief and practice. Both need to be emphasized. Correct belief makes you wise (3:15) and enables you to know truth and avoid myths (4:4). It includes careful instruction (4:2) and sound doctrine (4:3). Correct practice must not only be taught, but also reinforced with correction, rebuke, and instruction (3:16 and 4:2).

POWERFUL!—CHAPTER 3
Through Prayer

Acts 4:21-35

PERSPECTIVE: The Sanhedrin was the highest Jewish tribunal. Although Israel was subject to Rome, the Sanhedrin still judged in religious, civil, and criminal matters. They had authority to arrest, convict, and punish Jews. Under normal conditions they could not use capital punishment unless confirmed by the Romans. But in most cases this was little more than a rubber-stamp operation. If the Sanhedrin had concluded that Peter and John were misleading the Jews, that court could have requested the death sentence for the two apostles.

TEACHING OBJECTIVE: To realize that prayer can release God's power in us.

DISCUSSION IDEAS:
1. Some people have pointed to this passage, saying it promotes communistic and/or socialistic ideals. The voluntary sharing of possessions differs from any political system.

2. "Are you more likely to pray when things are going well or when they are going badly?"

   "What does this indicate about you?"

3. "What differences do you see between a person who requests things like the apostles did and a person who requests things like a new car?"

4. "All of us can grow in our understanding of God. Why will a more complete concept of God improve your prayers?"

5. "Why can you say that not seeing results from your prayers does not always mean you lack power in prayer?"

6. One purpose of this question is to show that power in prayer doesn't always result in a supernatural experience.

SUMMARY: After their brief stay in jail, Peter and John were warned not to talk about Jesus. The Church, knowing Peter and

John would not heed the warning, prayed for boldness. Four results of their prayer are recorded: the meeting place was shaken; the people were filled with the Holy Spirit; they proclaimed the resurrection of Jesus boldly; and the Church was characterized by extreme generosity and care for one another.

By His Spirit

Galatians 5:13-26

PERSPECTIVE: Paul wrote the letter to the church at Galatia primarily to correct a legalistic mentality. The people had developed the idea that salvation in Christ was only a beginning and they needed to maintain good works by human effort to have a right relationship with God (Galatians 3:1-3). Paul asserts that being right with God is not a result of works. This does not negate good morals, but means that they don't make you right with God. They are the fruit of the Spirit, not the means to a right relationship with God.

TEACHING OBJECTIVE: To know that God's Spirit empowers a person to live correctly.

DISCUSSION IDEAS:
1. "What, to you, are the most attractive aspects of the correct lifestyle presented in this chapter?"

4. To help the group discuss what this verse may mean, ask what law(s) we are not under. Some responses may be the Mosaic law, the Ten Commandments, the Levitical law, the Old Testament, the law of God, and civil law.

6. "If a person has peace but not gentleness, can he be walking in the Spirit?"

SUMMARY: Because you live in the Spirit, you should walk in the Spirit, not the flesh. The Spirit produces virtuous character, inward fulfillment, and a disciplined life. The flesh, to the contrary, is selfish, base, uncontrolled, and distasteful. As you keep in step with the Spirit, He empowers you to live the life you love.

POWERFUL!—CHAPTER 5
By Faith

Hebrews 11:1-12

PERSPECTIVE: Because the Book of Hebrews was written by a Hebrew to Hebrews, it is a difficult book for Gentiles to understand. Many Jews had come to Jesus, but began to suffer persecution. Naturally, they reasoned this way: "Before Jesus, we worshiped the true and living God and no one persecuted us. Now we worship the same God but we are persecuted. Let's return to the old form of worship."

Hebrews was written to encourage the Jewish believers to maintain their faith in Jesus Christ. Many examples of people who persevered in faith are given in chapter 11 as a stimulus to these Jews to persevere also.

TEACHING OBJECTIVE: To show that power through faith will carry you through hardships.

DISCUSSION IDEAS:

1. Read the following definitions after the group members give theirs.

   Faith: "PISTIS ... firm persuasion, a conviction based upon hearing (akin to *peitho*, to persuade). ...
   "The main elements in faith ... are (1) a firm conviction, ... (2) a personal surrender, ... (3) a conduct inspired by such surrender. ... All this stands in contrast to belief in its purely natural exercise, which consists of an opinion held in good faith without necessary reference to its proof."[1]

2. "What does it imply to you in knowing there are a variety of results of faith?"

3,4. Discuss each person studied, one at a time. Ask questions like, "What word from God did *Abel* have?" "How did the action(s) *Abel* took flow from his faith?" "How are we like *Abel*?" This will lead the discussion to question 4.

5. "Should we conclude that startling results are the correct

82

evidence of power through faith?" To relate your discussion to chapter 2, "By the Scriptures," ask, "What must be the object of our faith if we are to have power?"

SUMMARY: Faith is necessary to please God. There are numerous examples of God's power being released because of someone's faith: Enoch escaped death and Noah a catastrophe. Abel was accepted by the Lord and Abraham received power to father a nation. These examples are for our challenge, comfort, and instruction.

NOTE
1. *Vine's Expository Dictionary of New Testament Words* (Nashville, Tennessee: Royal Publishers, Inc., n.d.), page 401.

POWERFUL!—CHAPTER 6
To Persevere

2 Corinthians 4

PERSPECTIVE: When trials come and the temptation to give up enters our mind, we need the power to persevere. Evidently Paul had been experiencing trials and temptations just prior to writing this letter to the church at Corinth. He mentions various discouragements throughout the book: He was "under great pressure" (1:8) and "despaired even of life" (1:9); he experienced "anguish of heart" (2:4) and "no peace of mind" (2:13); he encountered "troubles, hardships and distresses" (6:4) and was "harassed at every turn" (7:5). Paul was qualified to speak of persevering.

TEACHING OBJECTIVE: To know that God will empower you to persevere no matter what discouragements you are facing.

DISCUSSION IDEAS:
1. "What are the benefits of persevering?"

   "Which of these ideas from question 1 have helped you persevere? How?"

2. Help your group see that everyone experiences discouragement. The dangers are allowing it to continue or letting it lead to wrong actions.

4. Because these expressions are figurative, a variety of meanings can be given to them. Don't expect unity in the answers or strive for a consensus. Allow freedom.

5. Ask, "What are some areas today in which Christians do not persevere?" Some answers are marriage, good works, church responsibilities, and giving. Then ask, "How do you think daily renewal from God would help people persevere in these areas?"

SUMMARY: To keep on keeping on, you must begin with integrity, purity, and humility. Look to God, not to your accomplishments. He will carry you through physical, mental, and emotional stress. Anticipate that you will relive Jesus' experience of seeing resurrection after death. Keep your perspective by not looking at your troubles but looking at things that cannot be seen with your eyes.

Through Cooperation

1 Corinthians 12:12-31

PERSPECTIVE: Paul's first letter to the church at Corinth reveals they were not experiencing power through cooperation. There were divisions among them: people were following different leaders (1:10-12); there was jealousy and quarreling (3:3); believers were suing one another in open court (6:1-6); they had different ideas regarding food (10:23-33); and there were divisions at the communion table (11:17-22). One purpose of Paul's letter was to correct these problems and to see the church gain power through cooperation.

TEACHING OBJECTIVE: To gain power from cooperation and unity in the church fellowship.

DISCUSSION IDEAS:

2. "What causes feelings of inferiority?"

   "What has helped you overcome feelings of inferiority?"

3. Some other Bible verses that can foster a positive and correct self-esteem:

   Genesis 1:26-27; we bear God's image.

   Romans 8:16-17; we are God's children.

   1 Corinthians 3:16; we are God's temple.

4. Some ideas to consider:

   The other parts of your body try to ease the pain.

   The other parts react to the toe, not to themselves.

   No other concern is important for the moment.

   The other parts take extra responsibility until the hurt member is healed.

5. Be careful to keep the discussion positive. Don't criticize

people or permit any gossip.

6. "What happens in a group when the fruit are emphasized?"

   "What happens in a group when gifts are emphasized?"

SUMMARY: The Body of Christ consists of people with a diversity of gifts and positions. No one is insignificant; all are essential. No one is independent; all are interdependent. Only through cooperation can the Body function properly. Then, any part that is honored causes all to rejoice.

POWERFUL!—CHAPTER 8
Over Sin

Romans 6

PERSPECTIVE: In Romans, Paul presents justification by faith. In chapter 5, he lists some of the implications of being justified. It means we will be delivered from God's wrath (5:9). We have peace *with* God (5:1). We were made righteous (5:19), and our sin is always surpassed by God's grace (5:20-21). But justification does not excuse us from striving against sin. Instead, it opens the door for power over sin.

TEACHING OBJECTIVE: To know the importance of gaining power over sin and the means of exercising that power.

DISCUSSION IDEAS:

1. Possible answers:

   1-4; Don't live in sin.

   5-7; Your old self was executed.

   8-10; You join in Jesus' resurrection.

   11-14; Don't let sin dominate you.

   15-18; Obeying sin leads to being a slave.

   19-23; Sin bears bitter fruit.

3. "What other reasons can you offer for not being passive about sin?"

4. "What attitudes lead to offering yourself to God?"

   "What attitudes lead to offering yourself to sin?"

5. "What reveals who you are enslaved to?"

SUMMARY: Grace that exceeds sin is no excuse to sin. Sinning doesn't make sense for us because our unity with Christ includes dying with Him and rising again. Our death is to sin. Our resurrection is to a new life. Further, sinning doesn't make sense because it will only enslave us to practices we detest.

Over the Devil

Matthew 4:1-11

PERSPECTIVE: The writer of Hebrews, in describing Jesus Christ, says He "has been tempted in every way, just as we are—yet was without sin" (4:15). Perhaps the writer was thinking of Jesus' temptation by the Devil, recorded in Matthew 4. Here Jesus behaves in a human manner. He doesn't demonstrate His divine authority over the Devil. He overcomes the Devil's temptations using the same resources available to you and me.

TEACHING OBJECTIVE: To know that power to overcome the Devil, demonstrated by Jesus, is available to us.

DISCUSSION IDEAS:
1. Ask, "In these events, do you see Jesus exercising super-human authority?" Help the group members see that at times He relied on the same resources available to you.

2. "Besides hunger, what are some other conditions that make you more susceptible to temptation?"

3. Some ideas to channel your thinking:

   Short-range solutions versus long-range solutions.

   The ends justify the means.

   Seeing is believing.

   Only what is logical to me could be true.

4. Ask, "What are some differences between stubbing your toe and jumping off a building?" The discussion will contrast God's protection against accidents with expecting safety in deliberate destructive acts.

5. "What are some circumstances that cause you to doubt God?"

   "What are some statements you hear that cause people to doubt God's ability or faithfulness?"

SUMMARY: The last two major events prior to Jesus' public ministry were His baptism by John and overcoming the Devil. Using the authority of the Scriptures, He proved the Devil's statements to be false and rejected his temptations. Then the Devil left and God sent angels to care for Jesus.

POWERFUL!—CHAPTER 10
Over Life's Trials

1 Peter 1:3-21

PERSPECTIVE: Peter recognized that people tend to be discouraged when they are assaulted. He suggests several actions to minimize persecution or to help you maintain a positive outlook. Besides those given in the study passage, he emphasizes maintaining an alien mindedness (2:11-12), obeying laws and rules (2:13-17), following Christ's example (2:18-25), seeking peace and harmony (3:8-12), keeping a clear conscience (3:15-17), having Christ's attitude (4:1-6), anticipating suffering (4:12-19), and remembering you're not alone (5:9).

TEACHING OBJECTIVE: To show how God's power is available to overcome the trials you are facing today.

DISCUSSION IDEAS:
1. Most people today are not facing the trials of homelessness, hunger, and persecution. Ask, "What are some of the trials we are facing?"

   "What, if any, trials are we facing *because* we're Christians?"

2. "Besides this passage, what other verses show that God's shielding power does not keep us from trials?"

5. Also see 1 Peter 2:11-12.

6. "What is the proper perspective of trials?"

SUMMARY: In Heaven everything will be perfect. In this life you face all kinds of trials. These trials both prove and refine your faith. To overcome in these trials requires a ready mind, disciplined life, and holy character. Since God has already paid the ultimate price for you, you need not worry whether or not He will protect His purchase.

To Testify

2 Timothy 1:7-18

PERSPECTIVE: Paul's second letter to Timothy was probably Paul's last letter. He was nearing death and he recognized its approach: "I am already being poured out like a drink offering, and the time has come for my departure. I have fought the good fight, I have finished the race, I have kept the faith" (2 Timothy 4:6-7). Both this expectation and the close relationship between Paul and Timothy reveal the importance and impact of the statements of this letter.

TEACHING OBJECTIVE: To recognize that God's power enables you to speak for Him.

DISCUSSION IDEAS:

1. After people have read their statements, ask, "How does this all fit together?" or "What does this mean to us today?"

2. One set of answers:

   Power; keeps me from experiencing shame because I'm in a position of authority.

   Love; being ashamed comes from focusing attention on myself. Love forces me to focus attention on others.

   Self-discipline; keeps me from allowing my emotions to rule my actions.

3. Instead of emphasizing countries where freedom is limited, discuss the repercussions people in your group may need to endure, such as social rejection, not being promoted, being misunderstood, etc.

4. Before discussing the questions in the study book, ask, "What is a major hindrance to you in presenting the gospel?"

6. Here are some ideas that can help foster in-depth discussion:

ACTIVITIES TO DEVELOP RELATIONSHIPS	ACTIVITIES THAT PREPARE ME	ACTIVITIES THAT LEAD TO PRESENTATION
Invite over for pie and coffee.	Write out testimony.	Invite to gospel movie.
Play tennis together.	Practice presenting gospel.	Give a book.
Do a favor for a person.		Tell my story.

SUMMARY: Never be ashamed to tell others about Jesus. He gives you power, not timidity. If you suffer because you testify, so what? He's able to take care of you. Be sure what you say about Him is true, whether you speak from the platform or in a private conversation. Don't abandon God's servants; they may need your help.

By Full Armor

Ephesians 6:10-20

PERSPECTIVE: This passage is the conclusion of the letter to the church at Ephesus, the church of whom God said, "You have persevered and have endured hardships for my name, and have not grown weary" (Revelation 2:3). Perhaps through receiving this very letter from Paul they were encouraged to press on with the courage and determination that would later result in this tribute from God.

TEACHING OBJECTIVE: To show that having God's power is the result of fulfilling all your responsibilities.

DISCUSSION IDEAS:

1. This exercise helps to foster an understanding of the verses. Emphasize understanding the main thoughts of the verses, not under which title they are listed.

2. "If you could actually see the desperate nature of the spiritual battle you are in, how do you think it would affect you?"

3. This question is likely to engender more discussion than there's time for. Break into small groups of three or four people to compare responses for ten minutes.

4. "What advantages are there to feeling strong and confident?"

5. As people discuss their answers, encourage others in the group to make suggestions. Ask, "What has helped you in this area?"

SUMMARY: Don't go running off half-cocked! Desperate battles require comprehensive equipment. Using all that is available means you'll still be standing when the smoke clears. Protect yourself with salvation, righteousness, and faith. Arm yourself with truth and the gospel. Be aggressive with the Word of God and your prayers. Then fearlessly attack as a representative of God Himself.

CHANGED!
REFLECTING YOUR LOVE FOR GOD

CHANGED!—CHAPTER 1
Renewed

Ephesians 4:17-32

PERSPECTIVE: This passage is the first study of *Changed!* because it mentions several specific areas that may require change and also gives a pattern for change. The pattern may be briefly stated as (1) recognize your need for change; (2) get the correct mindset; (3) replace vices with virtues; (4) discipline your actions.

TEACHING OBJECTIVE: To begin steps toward change in one area of life.

DISCUSSION IDEAS:

1. Below are some differences that help answer the second part of the question.

MORAL CONSCIOUSNESS	NEW SELF
Taught by parents, others	Taught by Christ (verses 20-21)
Like other people	Like God (verse 24)
Follows good examples	Follows Christ's example (verse 32)
Obeys own thinking	Obeys truth (verse 21)

2. Notice that in the replacement process of renewal there is a common element in the vice and the virtue. Speaking the truth replaces lying; both involve speaking. Generosity replaces stealing; both deal with money. Edification replaces vile conversation; both deal with speaking.

3. Be prepared to read your goal first as an example for the group.

4. Beware of trying to draw a fine line of when anger is sinful. Instead, ask, "What are the dangers of anger?" and then, "What mindset helps you keep anger from doing harm?"

5. One purpose of this question is to alert people to the influences that are bombarding them. Ask, "What are some

things you can do to keep these influences from leading you astray?"

SUMMARY: You are not to live like those who are insensitive to sin. You have a new nature that replaces the old. Put on this new self. Substitute generosity for thievery, the truth for lying, compassion for vengeance. Replace every sin with a virtue.

CHANGED!—CHAPTER 2
Loving

1 Corinthians 13

PERSPECTIVE: Undoubtedly, most of the people in your group will be familiar with 1 Corinthians 13. One danger of reviewing this passage is that the group may have the attitude, "I've already studied that." In this chapter, the goal is not so much acquiring new knowledge as learning *to love.*

First Corinthians 13 stands in the middle of a long section about spiritual gifts (chapters 12-14). Love, not the exercise of gifts, is shown to be "the most excellent way."

TEACHING OBJECTIVE: To love more.

DISCUSSION IDEAS:

1. It is unlikely that group members will have significantly different answers to this question. Ask them to close their eyes and think about their lives as you *slowly* read the lists. (Pause two or three seconds after each word or phrase.) Then ask, "What came to your mind as I read these lists?"

3. A press release is usually a short statement written for publication that lists the qualities of a person or product.

4. "What have you observed when people exercise gifts without love?"

   "Can a person love others on a consistent basis for any length of time without using his or her gift(s)?"

6. Don't spend much time on the problems; concentrate on the solutions. Ask the group to evaluate this response: "The best suggestion I have to help others be more loving is for me to love them."

SUMMARY: Love validates actions. True love always focuses on the interests of others. Doing everything for their comfort and benefit, expecting nothing in return—this love always succeeds. It is *the* great virtue.

Humble

Philippians 2:1-11

PERSPECTIVE: Humility is one of the most difficult virtues to discuss. One person said, "Once you think you have it, you lose it." Paul's statements later in Philippians seem to indicate he understood the difficulty in having a humble attitude. In 3:4-6 he tells of his position and accomplishments. Then he says he considers them rubbish (verse 8). He goes on to say in verse 13, "I do not consider myself yet to have taken hold of it" (Christ's purpose for him). Humility is having an accurate attitude toward yourself.

TEACHING OBJECTIVE: To express humility in relationship to God and others.

DISCUSSION IDEAS:
1. "If you're not experiencing the conditions mentioned in verse 1, what should be done to remedy this situation?"

2. "Which condition do you find most difficult to comply with?"

3. "What did Jesus do that showed He considered others better?"

    "What should you do?"

4. Note that Jesus did not consider Himself to be "bad" or "unfit" or to have any other negative qualities.

6. "What is likely to happen if you have a poor self-image?"

7. Ask the group how the study passage reinforces their answers.

SUMMARY: Jesus is the perfect example of humility. He knew who He was, but assumed a low position as a servant and a condemned criminal. We, too, should know who we are in Christ. Then, being willing to assume a lesser position, we should act in the interest of others.

Generous

2 Corinthians 9

PERSPECTIVE: The first letter to the church at Corinth is a sharp reproof from Paul dealing with dissention, adultery, drunkenness (at communion), and other blatant problems. Evidently, the church took these reproofs to heart and repented (2 Corinthians 7:8-9). In his second letter, Paul addresses the need to be generous, not so much because it is a problem, but because it is a virtue.

TEACHING OBJECTIVE: To give generously and with the right attitudes.

DISCUSSION IDEAS:
1. "What significance do you see in these different expressions?"
2. "What are some wrong motivations for giving?"

   "How should we respond to wrong motivations?"
4. "What should we do if we have wrong attitudes?"
5. "Does all grace mean that we will always be financially prosperous?"
6. "From all we've learned about generosity, what new insight do you have regarding Jesus' statement, 'Where your treasure is, there your heart will be also'?"

SUMMARY: Wow! We get to give. What a privilege! We can show our love and care. We can help others. We can reflect God's great gift to us. On top of all this, our generosity yields bountiful rewards.

CHANGED!—CHAPTER 5
Submissive

1 Peter 2:13-25

PERSPECTIVE: Peter wrote this letter to encourage a suffering church to persevere. Most contemporary minds would picture the "perseverer" as a rugged individualist prepared to defend his rights. In contrast, Peter presents the need to be submissive. Such submissiveness should not be mistaken for passiveness. As you will study in the next chapter, submission often is bold and courageous.

TEACHING OBJECTIVE: To actively submit to authorities.

DISCUSSION IDEAS:

1. Instead of having members of the group read their lists of commands, ask individuals to tell which command is particularly difficult to fulfill.

2. Focus the discussion on reasons to submit. Avoid discussing situations in which you should not submit. (You will study this in the next chapter.)

3. Integrate the discussion of this question with question 6 by asking, "How can we live as free men in situation 1 of question 6?"

    "How can we live as servants in this situation?"

4. "What examples of suffering for doing good are you aware of?"

SUMMARY: Submit to people in authority as though they were the Lord. Obey civil law and your boss at work—even if he is overbearing and unreasonable. Be like Jesus. He suffered the ultimate injustice without any cross words or accusations. By submitting to cruel punishment, He redeemed your soul.

CHANGED!—CHAPTER 6
Uncompromising

Daniel 6

PERSPECTIVE: Daniel was a man of conviction who wouldn't compromise, but he was not unmanageable or unaccommodating. Earlier he had resolved not to eat the king's food. He didn't just say, "No, I won't!" Instead, he proposed eating vegetables for ten days. The official, with some reservations, agreed and was pleased to see that this diet only improved Daniel and his friends. He suggested a reasonable alternative in one case, but in Daniel 6 he was uncompromising.

TEACHING OBJECTIVE: To recognize that you should not compromise on convictions in order to submit to an authority.

DISCUSSION IDEAS:
1. "What would be a modern-day parallel to Daniel and his position?"
2. "Why do you suppose these men acted so deviously?"

   "Why do many people behave like these governors?"
4. Be sure the discussion considers both positive and negative effects on people.
5. "What do these two different examples mean for us today?"
6. Review the situations presented in question 6 of the previous chapter and ask, "Now that we've studied about being uncompromising, would you change your answer to question 6?"

SUMMARY: It is not uncommon for unrighteous men to seek a grievance against righteous people. To vent their displeasure, wicked men often use unreasonable rules. If no alternative to such a rule is available, conviction demands that we ignore it. God may or may not rescue us from the ensuing penalties, but by not compromising, we place ourselves in His keeping.

CHANGED!—CHAPTER 7

Careful in Speech

James 3:1-12

PERSPECTIVE: The Book of James is sometimes called "Proverbs of the New Testament" because it contains so many maxims for practical daily living. It does not present much theology. But James is thorough in explaining how we should use our tongues.

TEACHING OBJECTIVE: To reduce the quantity of words and increase the quality of them.

DISCUSSION IDEAS:
2. Encourage specific responses. A general response such as "be careful" doesn't foster much discussion. A response such as, "I'd open doors carefully, look about the room before entering, and then not stand near any potential hiding place for the snake," can lead to some interesting parallels to speech.

3. "One important reason not to degrade others, even in jest, is that a mild comment may be perceived as a severe blow. A common practice today is to ridicule your spouse. What attitude fosters this behavior?"

4. "Imagine you own an apple orchard. One of your trees is producing fruit that has a bad taste. But both the tree and the fruit look fine. Further study of the tree confirms there is no disease or fungus. What will you check next? How is this tree like people?"

SUMMARY: Teaching is an awesome responsibility because it is easy to say the wrong thing—and words can be devastating. It's virtually impossible to control your tongue. You end up saying conflicting things. You should speak in praise to God and never curse anyone.

CHANGED!—CHAPTER 8
Forgiving

Matthew 18:21-35

PERSPECTIVE: Peter's question about forgiveness reflects new thinking for him. Jewish tradition was to forgive three times and then apply the "eye-for-an eye" principle. But Peter had heard Jesus talk about a person not asserting his rights. He probably was trying to figure out exactly how often Jesus intended this response to apply.

TEACHING OBJECTIVE: To forgive *all* people for *all* offenses.

DISCUSSION IDEAS:

1. The purpose of this question is to give an overview of the passage. Don't spend much time discussing responses. Each part is amplified in the rest of the questions. Question 2 refers to the principle; questions 3 and 4, the illustration; questions 5-7, the application.

2. Additional references regarding this point are Matthew 6:12 and Luke 17:3-4. Ask, "Do you really want God to treat you as you have treated others?"

3. "Is it fair to compare my sins to a $2,000,000 debt and other people's sins against me to a $20 debt?"

5. "What should you say to a sweet grandmother who says, 'I've tried to forgive him for what he's done, but I can't'?"

    "Do we always have power to forgive another person?"

6. You can develop this question further by helping the group members see that when they are unforgiving, they harm themselves, not the person who needs to be forgiven. The unforgiving get ulcers, suffer from poor digestion, experience mental anguish, and so on.

SUMMARY: Always forgive. No matter what offense you suffer from another, it's a drop in the bucket compared to your offenses against God. He's forgiven you all your sins; you should forgive others for everything else.

Pure

1 Thessalonians 4:1-12

PERSPECTIVE: How to "know God's will" is a popular topic among Christians, especially concerning who to marry, what career to pursue, or where to live. The Bible gives direction on how to make these decisions, but you may not find specific answers. However, there is clear definition of God's will for your life in one area. In the study passage, Paul asserts and reasserts that your purity is God's will.

TEACHING OBJECTIVE: To recognize impurity and abstain from it.

DISCUSSION IDEAS:
1. "One characteristic of a pure person is that he is 'sexually' moral. What does this mean?" (Verses that may help answer this question are Exodus 20:14, Romans 1:27, and Hebrews 13:4.)

2. All these verses deal with the concept that the command for purity comes from God, by His will and by His authority.

3. Ask the group to first list the qualities stated in verses 9-12. Then have them "read between the lines" and tell what other qualities are implied. Finally, repeat the question from the chapter.

4. Be careful not to judge others' actions as wrong unless the Bible says they are wrong. Instead, direct the discussion toward ways of avoiding temptation.

5. "How do you benefit by maintaining a pure life?"

SUMMARY: By the authority of God and according to His will, you are commanded to be pure from sexual immorality. Control your passion. Channel your energy into true love and hard work.

Sensitive

Romans 14

PERSPECTIVE: One reason some Christians did not approve of eating meat was the questionable method of obtaining it. Many pagan ceremonies of idol or demon worship included sacrificing animals. Afterward, the clean-up crew would sell these carcasses to local butchers at reduced rates. Many Christians felt it was not proper to eat meat that had been sacrificed to the Devil. To avoid this possibility, they didn't eat it at all.

TEACHING OBJECTIVE: To recognize the validity of others' opinions and act in sensitivity to their beliefs.

DISCUSSION IDEAS:

1. Have two or three people read what they have underlined (and only that) without discussing their reasons. These ideas will come out later as you discuss all the material.

2. "Who would be a weak or strong person today?"

3. "What are some issues today about which Christians have differing views?"

4. "Can you think of any other reasons?"

5. "We've just been talking about the principles followed by a sensitive person. What does a sensitive person *do* about the issue of . . . ?" (Fill in the blank in a way that will help group members.)

6. Spend some time discussing examples that relate to the people in your group.

SUMMARY: We should accept other believers, even if they have different opinions. We shouldn't make fun of them for being "too narrow" or criticize them for being "too liberal." We are individually responsible to God. Rather than flaunting our freedom, we can do things that will promote love and growth.

A Good Family Member

Ephesians 5:15-6:4

PERSPECTIVE: One purpose of the Book of Ephesians was to correct the prejudice that existed against Gentiles. Many Jews who had become Christians felt they were better than the "pagan Gentiles" even after they became Christians too. Paul asserts that Christ "made the two [Jew and Gentile] one and has destroyed the barrier [between them]" (Ephesians 2:14). Unity in Christ is also the foundation for good family relationships. Moreover, good families produce a society free of prejudice and discrimination.

TEACHING OBJECTIVE: To know your family responsibilities and to do them.

DISCUSSION IDEAS:
3. "What evidence can you offer that God does not intend for a wife to 'live in the shadow' of her husband?"

5. "What are some ways to honor our parents day by day?"

   "What is one special activity you can do to honor your parents?"

6. "What are some specific actions you have taken to help train your children properly?"

WARNING: Marriage relationships and child rearing are topics that require vast amounts of time to understand and apply. You cannot be thorough and maintain your study schedule. You must make a "quick pass" at this time.

SUMMARY: Good family relationships develop from lives that are filled with the Spirit. Marriages are built on love and submission patterned after Christ and the Church. Children are cooperative, not rebellious. Parents provide wisdom.

CHANGED!—CHAPTER 12
Worshipful

Psalm 145

PERSPECTIVE: The attitudes and actions of worship seem to be "caught" more than taught. So, instead of reviewing passages that tell about the need for, aspects of, and ways to worship, you are studying the example of David's worship. Psalm 145 is one of many psalms of worship. In fact, most of the questions in this chapter can be used for other psalms of worship.

The topic of worship was chosen as the last chapter in this book because as you experience positive changes in your life, a natural response is to worship God for the great work He has done in you.

TEACHING OBJECTIVE: To worship God in spirit and in truth.

DISCUSSION IDEAS:
Rather than discuss the answers in your book, spend your time worshiping God. Develop a plan for your time together from the suggestions below. Don't be "locked into" your plan, but follow it with sensitivity to God's leading.

1. *Praise time*—Have people pray one-sentence praises to God. Don't go around the circle, but pray in random order. People can pray as often as they wish, but only one sentence each time. It may go something like this:

    "I praise you for your greatness."

    "I love you."

    "You are so wonderful to us."

2. *Song time*—Sing songs that are meaningful to your group. Perhaps you could play a praise album and sing with it.

3. *Scripture reading*—Ask everyone to close their eyes and meditate on God's Word as one person slowly reads Psalm 145.

4. *Mutual appreciation*—God is glorified by unity and love in

His Body. Have everybody in the group tell what is special about the person on his or her right.

SUMMARY: Worship the Lord with praise and adoration. Worship Him for His mighty deeds and powerful acts. Worship Him for His love and kindness. Tell others of His compassion and mercy. He will uphold you, protect you and provide for you. He deals righteously and justly with all people. Worship Him with all creation.

FULFILLED!

ENJOYING GOD'S PURPOSE FOR YOU

Offering Yourself

Romans 11:33-12:21

PERSPECTIVE: Most of the epistles written by Paul contain a pivotal verse. It marks a change of emphasis from doctrine to application. Basically, it means, "Since all this is true, here's how it should affect your life." Romans 12:1 is the pivot in Romans. Previously, Paul explained God's grace and mercy when He justified you by faith apart from works. In 12:1, Paul turns to application. He urges you, in light of this fantastic mercy, to offer yourself to God.

TEACHING OBJECTIVE: To recognize that the only reasonable action to take is total surrender to God.

DISCUSSION IDEAS:

2. "What other reasons for offering yourself to God can you think of?"

3. There are no clear statements in the Bible that tell how to identify your gifts, but the following questions have been helpful to many people:

   What do I enjoy doing?

   What do I do well?

   What do others like to have me do?

4. There does not appear to be a focus for these commands. They involve your relationships to others and to yourself, your attitudes and your deeds, your private life and your public life, your actions and your reactions.

5. "How have you applied these concepts to your work relationships? To your spouse? To your church?"

SUMMARY: God is so great, so good, and so merciful that you have only one rational response: give yourself to Him. Don't act like everyone else. Think with God. Be honest about yourself. Be loving toward others. Be enthusiastic in everything. Let forgiveness, not vengeance, control you.

Working Together

Ephesians 4:1-16

PERSPECTIVE: The letter to the Ephesians was written to combat prejudice and inequality in the church. Many Jews considered themselves superior to Gentiles because Jews had been God's people for two millennia. It was hard for them to accept that in Christ both Jew and Gentile were one; that is, that God did not discriminate between them. In Ephesians, Paul asserts that we *need* one another.

TEACHING OBJECTIVE: To show the purpose and benefits of church unity.

DISCUSSION IDEAS:

1. "How do verses 11 and 12 present one way we work together?"

   "What is helping you have these attitudes?"

2. "What changes would occur if we really applied this passage to our churches today?"

   "How can we begin to make these changes?"

5. Many people find it difficult to talk about their strong points as mature Christians. Rather than do that, have members of the group point out evidences of Christian maturity they see in each other.

SUMMARY: We are one in Christ but diverse in capacity and position. God has gifted some to be leaders. They equip and coach the others to perform spiritual service. God designed His Church to work together like a fine-tuned piece of machinery. This amazing machine is equipped for self-maintenance, self repair, and automatic adjustments. And it still has power for high-level productivity.

FULFILLED!—CHAPTER 3
Helping Others Grow

1 Thessalonians 2:1-12

PERSPECTIVE: Paul, Silas, and Timothy were the main leaders who founded the church at Thessalonica. After three weeks of explaining the death, burial, and resurrection of Jesus, and how those events were prophesied in the Old Testament, they persuaded some Jews and a large number of Greeks that Jesus was the Messiah. Jealous Jews incited a riot, resulting in the arrest of Paul's host, Jason. The church then encouraged Paul to go on to other cities. It is uncertain how long Paul, Silas, and Timothy had stayed in Thessalonica. It was definitely at least one month and may have been five or six months.

TEACHING OBJECTIVE: For every person to know that he or she can help others grow spiritually.

DISCUSSION IDEAS:
1. "Which actions can we take also?"

   "If we are not able to do everything Paul did, will we be able to help others?"

2. "In the spiritual context, what is milk?"

   "How do we feed others?"

   "What differences are there between breast feeding and bottle feeding?"

3. "What is the first step in meeting your challenge?"

4. "Has anybody shared his life with you in this manner?"

5. Present all of these questions at once:

   "Does God really expect us to operate as these descriptions suggest?"

   "If not, what does God expect of us?"

   "If so, how do we start to do it?"

SUMMARY: "Despite obstacles, we diligently worked to teach you spiritual truth. We were honest with you, with ourselves and with God. At times we acted like your mother — tender and compassionate; other times like your father — stern and challenging. But we always acted with your best interests at heart."

Balancing Your Faith
James 2:14-24

PERSPECTIVE: James, a practical man, wrote about the daily behavior of people. To him, the ultimate test of religion was how it affected your work, your family, and your conduct. His pragmatic approach to Christianity may lead you to think that he lacked depth. This passage demonstrates his understanding of the Scriptures, as he cites examples from the Old Testament to illustrate his teachings.

TEACHING OBJECTIVE: To show the importance of works as an evidence of true faith.

DISCUSSION IDEAS:
1. Emphasize the third part of this question by asking, "Since this is an important subject today, what should we do about it?"

2. "What do you think James would say to you if you told a person in need that you'd pray for him?"

3. "What would be an experience similar to Abraham's for a person today?"

4. One person has said, "It is by faith alone that we are saved, but the faith that saves is never alone."

5. The general answer to this question is established in Luke 6:46 – obedience. Have your group go on to list specific actions, such as forgiving others, loving others, turning the other cheek.

SUMMARY: Genuine faith is always accompanied by actions. It is easy to say you believe, but deeds verify your claim. Abraham not only said he believed God, but also demonstrated the depth of his faith when he "sacrificed" Isaac.

Caring Enough to Act

Matthew 25:14-46

PERSPECTIVE: Both the Gospel of John and the Gospel of Matthew detail the last week of Jesus' life. But John recorded primarily the private talks Jesus had with the Twelve; Matthew recorded Jesus' public talks to a broad audience. John recorded words of peace and comfort; Matthew, the seven woes. In John, Heaven is a place prepared for you; in Matthew, the future includes judgment, as described in the study passage.

TEACHING OBJECTIVE: To take action toward people who need food, shelter, or comfort.

DISCUSSION IDEAS:

1. "What do you think the 'one-talent' man was afraid would happen?"

2. "The parable does not mention the possibility of a servant investing the money and losing it. What do you think the master would say in that situation?"

3. "The servants were given responsibilities proportional to their ability to handle them. Is that true of your responsibilities? If yes, what does that imply about how you function? If no, what should you do?"

5. "Is your service greater if you actually do the deed (such as feed the hungry) rather than give money to a program that does it?"

6. "Do we serve people if we meet their physical needs but fail to present the gospel?"

7. "What do the questions asked by the righteous in verses 37-39 indicate about their character?"

SUMMARY: God will give you responsibility according to your ability to handle it. He expects you to be a good steward of your abilities and responsibilities. Even when your responsibilities grow, be sure not to neglect the poor, the hungry, the sick, and others in need.

FULFILLED!—CHAPTER 6
Praying as a Body

Acts 12:1-19

PERSPECTIVE: This passage mentions several details about the way Peter was guarded in prison. There were "four squads of four soldiers each." The Romans divided the night into four three-hour segments. Each squad took one of these watches, two men with Peter and two men at the gates.

A prisoner was chained by his right wrist to the left wrist of a soldier. This allowed the guard to have his right arm free in case the prisoner attempted to escape. For greater security, as with Peter, the prisoner was chained to two soldiers, one on each side. Prayer alone broke through this rigid security.

TEACHING OBJECTIVE: To show the power and effectiveness of corporate prayer.

DISCUSSION IDEAS:
1. "Although we are very different from Herod, what characteristics of his do you think might creep into our lives if we are not careful?"

2. Some details to consider:

   Peter was sleeping.

   He was bound in chains.

   He wasn't wearing his clothes.

4. "How are you like these people?"

   "In what ways do you want to be more like them?"

SUMMARY: After executing James, Herod imprisoned Peter. The church gathered to offer prayers for his release. After weeks of prayer, God delivered Peter at the last moment, and he returned to their fellowship.

Telling Your Story

John 9

PERSPECTIVE: The ninth chapter of John sheds light on one of the great questions of philosophy: How can a God of love allow pain and suffering? Some assume that suffering is proportional to sin. The disciples' question in verse 2 reveals this logic. Jesus' response in verse 3 shows that the assumption is false. He turns this tragedy into a triumph by healing the man so he can tell others of his deliverance.

If we generalize this example, we might say that the purpose of suffering is to be delivered from it or taken through it by God so we can tell others our story.

TEACHING OBJECTIVE: To know that you have an interesting story that you should tell to others.

DISCUSSION IDEAS:

1. "People were interested in this man's story, probably because he had been healed of blindness. Many of us have not had such a dramatic experience, so what will cause others to be interested in our stories?"

2. "What are some dangers we face in communication because we know so much about Jesus, God, the Church, and doctrine?"

3. Consider the following elements in your discussion: attitudes, language, relationships, and activities that open opportunities to speak.

4. As you read your stories, use the elements for effectiveness discussed in question 3 to critique one another.

5. "What actions can you take to increase your sphere of influence?"

SUMMARY: A man healed of his blindness set an example for all of us. He freely and repeatedly told others what Jesus did for him. He could not argue eloquently, he did not understand Jesus fully, and he had no influential position. Yet he affected his community even to the level of the religious leaders.

FULFILLED!—CHAPTER 8
Telling His Story

Romans 10:1-15

PERSPECTIVE: Paul, a Jew, was the apostle to the Gentiles. Naturally, there were those who thought he had turned his back on the Jews. They felt he should give more effort to those who had been God's people for so long. Paul explained his actions:

> His mission was to the Gentiles (Galatians 2:9).
> The Jews stumbled over faith in Jesus (Romans 9:31-33).
> The Gentiles had been grafted into the places left bare by broken-off branches (Romans 11:17-21).
> He still had a passion for the Jews (Romans 10:1).

TEACHING OBJECTIVE: To motivate people to tell others about Jesus Christ.

DISCUSSION IDEAS:

2. People are likely to be confused by verses 6 and 7. Evidently, these were questions people asked in Paul's time, but were not the issue. In verse 8, he emphasizes what we should be talking about.

3. "What do you think Paul meant by 'preaching' in verse 14?" "In what sense should we preach? In what sense should we not preach?"

4. "What in the Great Commission makes you want to tell other people about Jesus?"

5. As the leader, give the group members an example to follow. Tell them who you are praying for, what you have done and are doing to build a relationship with him or her, what opportunities you've had to tell your story, what opportunities you've had to tell Jesus' story, and what your plans are.

SUMMARY: As it was for Paul, both your desire and prayer should be for the salvation of others. Even those who have religious zeal may need saving.

The message you are to proclaim is righteousness by faith in Jesus Christ. You should present His death and resurrection. As people believe and confess Jesus Christ as their Lord, they gain salvation. They need to hear the message from us, and we are blessed as we convey it to them.

Working Behind the Scenes

Acts 6:1-7

PERSPECTIVE: On the day of Pentecost, about 3,000 people were added to the Church. Not long afterward, Peter and John met a crippled man at the temple and Peter healed him. Peter used this opportunity to proclaim Jesus and many believed, "and the number of men grew to about five thousand" (Acts 4:4). These new converts came from all over. Fifteen countries are listed in Acts 2:9-11. Evidently, many of these people did not return home but stayed in Jerusalem. This gave rise to problems and the need for people to work behind the scenes.

TEACHING OBJECTIVE: To show that working behind the scenes is an elevated position necessary for the good of the Body.

DISCUSSION IDEAS:
1. "What are some similar needs we face in our church?"

2. "If we applied the same standards today, we might not have enough workers. What should we do?"

3. "Should everyone have a behind-the-scenes ministry?"

4. "Why do you think some people continue in behind-the-scenes ministries throughout their lives?"

   "What are some of the best ways to prepare yourself for a behind-the-scenes ministry?"

   "What are some of the best ways to prepare yourself for a public ministry?"

SUMMARY: Some of the first men to work behind the scenes in the Church corrected inequities in food distribution. Today, we may call a similar project "kitchen detail." These men, willing to accept a menial job, elevated the position of all who work behind the scenes. It is a league whose numbers include Stephen and Philip.

Serving 'Til It Hurts
Mark 10:23-45

PERSPECTIVE: Jesus' prophecy in verse 39 that the disciples would drink of His cup was fulfilled rather quickly after His death. James was the first apostle to be martyred. Herod Agrippa I ordered his death in approximately AD 44. John lived a long life, but much of it was spent in exile on the island of Patmos.

TEACHING OBJECTIVE: To make commitments to serve others even if it hurts.

DISCUSSION IDEAS:
1. "Jesus promised that those who have left people and things for the gospel will receive a hundred times as much in return. Do you think we should leave people and things in order to gain this hundredfold reward?"

2. "Do you think the disciples understood what Jesus was saying in verses 33 and 34? Why?"

4. "What is involved in being a slave of all?"

   "Should we serve nonChristians? If so, how?"

   Closing: "When should we say no to doing these jobs?"

SUMMARY: Riches can be the biggest obstacle to your spiritual health. Those who sacrifice anything for the sake of Christ will be justly rewarded.

Jesus set an example of sacrifice by dying for us on the Cross. In this way, He served others, not Himself. We should also serve others.

Qualifying as a Leader

1 Timothy 3

PERSPECTIVE: Paul wrote to Timothy almost 2000 years ago about directing the affairs of a local assembly. The same directives apply today. In summary, Paul said:

> Refute false teachers (chapter 1).
> Pray for the people (chapter 2).
> Appoint qualified leaders (chapter 3).
> Teach correct doctrine (chapter 4).
> Relate properly to all people (chapter 5).
> Don't let money ensnare you (chapter 6).

The study passage considers the high qualifications for leaders. These demanding characteristics are somewhat amazing when you consider the fact that being a church leader was a potential hazard. Many were beaten, banished, imprisoned, and sometimes killed. No doubt, both Paul and Timothy understood an unspoken requisite for leadership—courage!

TEACHING OBJECTIVE: To know the requisites for leadership in the church.

DISCUSSION IDEAS:

1. Ask, "In our church, what do we call the people who function as overseers and deacons?" Make sure your group relates the discussion of this chapter to positions in your church.

2. "What can happen in a church if these qualities are ignored?"

4. "Is there any difference between the requirements for leadership in the church and the measure of maturity for all Christians?"

6. This may have been an early creed that leaders recited.

SUMMARY: It is good to prepare yourself for spiritual responsibilities. Before he is given responsibility in the church, a person must have a pure character and a good reputation. He should demonstrate good leadership in his home. When the right kind of people are chosen as leaders, the whole church will benefit.

FULFILLED!—CHAPTER 12
Reaching to Other Nations
Acts 11

PERSPECTIVE: In the Old Testament, the Israelites were God's people; He was their God. In their minds, the Messiah was their Messiah, sent to deliver them. The first Christians were all Jews who thought Jesus, the Christ, would restore the nation of Israel. They could barely conceive the idea of allowing non-Jews into their numbers, much less the concept of actively pursuing fellowship with Gentiles. This was the thinking of those that God convinced to reach out to other nations.

TEACHING OBJECTIVE: To show that we must maintain mission mindedness.

DISCUSSION IDEAS:
1. "For someone today, what experience would parallel a Jew eating reptiles or nonkosher food?"

2. You may need to use additional questions to probe the effect of prejudice. For example, ask, "How do you think prejudice affects fund raising? Relationships to missionaries? Where we go?"

3. "If you were going to draw a map of the area you wish to influence for Jesus Christ, what would it look like?"

5. "How does our church reach out to our neighborhood? To our city? To our state?"

6. Missionaries in foreign lands often tell of the encouragement that letters and prayers bring. Challenge each person in your group to make a project of praying for and writing to one missionary on a consistent basis.

SUMMARY: Those who objected to Peter's consorting with Gentiles changed their minds when they heard about Peter's vision and how he was directed to Cornelius. Once the door to the Gentiles was opened, people began traveling to tell about Jesus and His resurrection. Stephen talked to Greeks, and Barnabas and Saul to the people at Antioch.

Celebrate!
Exalting God in Praise and Worship

CELEBRATE!—CHAPTER 1
For He Is Creator

Psalm 104

PERSPECTIVE: While plenty of people believe the universe occurred by chance, the Bible asserts they are deliberately closing their eyes to the obvious (Romans 1:20-21). The universe is no accident, but a masterpiece created by a supreme genius. And just as the author is greater than the book, so the Artist who made everything far surpasses everything He has made. He has endowed us with the ability to appreciate the wonder of His creation so that we can celebrate His work. Acknowledging Him as Creator is one of the foundation stones of our worship.

TEACHING OBJECTIVE: To praise God the Creator as you appreciate His works.

DISCUSSION IDEAS:

The objective of the leader's guide for *Celebrate!* is to integrate discussion about praise and worship with actually praising and worshiping God. Select some ideas that seem helpful.

1. Have the people in your group address their answers to God like this: "God you are. . . ." In this way each person will be offering a sentence of praise to God.

2. Ask group members what emotions these observations raise in them.

3. Offer God a sentence of thanks for His minute care of creation.

4. A light year is the distance light travels in one year or approximately nine trillion miles. Scientists have identified thousands of stars over 100 million light years away or 900,000,000,000,000,000,000 miles away. Another way to look at it is that what we see when we view these stars is what happened 100 million years ago.

   Ask group members to address their answers to God.

5. Tell what this experience was like for you. Have you ever done this before? Are you the kind of person who takes nature walks very often?

7. As far as we know, humans are the only part of creation on earth that appreciates beauty, can recognize the magnitude of God's power, or experiences feelings like wonder and awe. All of these thoughts help to humble and uplift us.

SUMMARY: As the saying goes, we should "take time to smell the roses" or notice the sunset or listen to the birds because these things remind us of our Creator watching over and caring for us.

For He Is Majestic
Psalm 18

PERSPECTIVE: The immensity of creation is a first peek at the greatness of God. But His majesty extends beyond creation. He is great in His love, His faithfulness, His deeds, His power, and every other way. His all-surpassing majesty goes beyond comprehension and imagination. It is at once terrifying and comforting, as David portrays in this psalm. When we see even a glimpse of God's true majesty, we can't help but fall to our knees in worship.

TEACHING OBJECTIVE: To sense the majesty of God and worship Him in His majesty.

DISCUSSION IDEAS:
1. Forces of nature come to most people's minds first, and those are the images David uses in verses 7-15 of his psalm. But the moral qualities we see in Scripture and experience from Him—His patience, repeated forgiveness, self-sacrifice, loyalty, justice—display a greatness beyond mere raw power.

   Take a minute to praise God for some of the things you name.
2. Do you worry that God is against you like this?
3. Thank God for being this kind of protector for you.
4. Answers to this question may be kept private.
6. Express your answers as praise to God.
7. What are some of the obstacles you face? Does thinking about God's majesty give you confidence?

SUMMARY: When we look at the heavens or the forces of nature, we can see God's majesty. When we remember history and what He has done for us personally, we can see His majesty. When we look inside ourselves, we can see His majesty. All that is in us should praise His majestic name.

For He Is Holy

1 Chronicles 16:8-36

PERSPECTIVE: A third foundational reason for worshiping God is His character. One of the central features of His character is holiness. If God were not holy, our lives would be nothing more than a cruel joke. But a Holy God could give us existence only if there were high purposes for our lives. David wrote this psalm of praise shortly after ascending to the throne of Israel, fulfilling one of the purposes of his life. His initial series of battlefield victories enabled him to bring the ark of the covenant to Jerusalem for a special time of celebration.

TEACHING OBJECTIVE: To sense the holiness of God and our unworthiness to come before Him.

DISCUSSION IDEAS:

1. In Old Testament times the tabernacle and the temple contained the Holy of Holies, where God dwelt. What do you know about the Holy of Holies that shows how sacred it was? (See, for example, Leviticus 16 and Hebrews 9:1-10.)

   How can we integrate the same sense of holiness that the Israelites had into our worship today?

2. What else stimulates you to worship God for His holiness?

3. Use participants' answers in a time of worship. Invite them each to express their feelings to God: "When I consider your holy authority, I feel. . . ."

4. In 1 Corinthians 7:5, Paul indicates that one form of offering for married couples could be abstaining from sex for a period. Fasting is a time-honored expression of worship. This concept can be generalized into abstaining from any pleasure as a sacrificial worship to God. Challenge the members of your group to select some legitimate pleasure to forego for one week, such as television, desserts, or recreational sports.

5,6. First discuss question 6 to gather ideas for incorporating the telling of God's acts in worship. Then use one or more of these ideas as a forum for people to tell of the acts of God they listed in question 5.

7. How do you feel about God when you envision this? How do you feel about yourself?

9. Go around the group two or three times using the following format. The first person will say, "Thank you God for ... " and read one of his or her answers. Then the whole group will respond, "We thank you, God." Then the next person will do likewise.

SUMMARY: The holiness of God is the basic reason why we worship Him, and the sense of holiness should be part of our worship.

The Incarnation

Luke 1:39-80

PERSPECTIVE: Christmas everyday may be a childhood fantasy for many, but in one sense it can be a reality for you. Christmas is the day we set aside as the anniversary of the birth of Jesus Christ, the day God entered the human realm as a human being. We can celebrate this incarnation daily in praise and worship.

TEACHING OBJECTIVE: To worship God for the Incarnation at Christmas and throughout the year.

DISCUSSION IDEAS:
1. After many reasons are given for celebrating the Incarnation, ask, "How can we celebrate the Incarnation more often than just at Christmas?"

2. Give everyone in the group an opportunity to read their amplified statements as praise to God.

3. Sing one stanza each of several of the carols suggested by participants. Also ask, "What are some of the songs often sung at Christmas that do not present correct Christmas ideals?"

4. This question provides a good opportunity for mini-drama. Have people give their responses as though they were there. For example, someone might start, "I live next door to Zechariah, and when. . . ."

6. How could you express one of those themes in celebration of the Incarnation in some way other than words (such as making a picture, banner, or other object; or through dance or mime)?

7. In the Old Testament, many of the blessings fathers offered for newborn children were in the form of prophecy telling what the child was to become. Is it appropriate for us to imitate their example? If so, how? If not, why not?

137

SUMMARY: Under the New Covenant, the first great event we celebrate is the Incarnation. It opens the door to knowing God: first by seeing Him in our form; second by providing reconciliation through His body.

The Cross

1 Corinthians 11:17-34

PERSPECTIVE: Like most of Paul's letters, the one to the church at Corinth was sent to correct some problems. The problems in this church were legion and severe, and this letter stands out as a strict and harsh one. In one case regarding sexual immorality, Paul even said to hand the offender over to Satan.

It is obvious from the study passage that the problems affected one of the most solemn rites of Christianity: the Lord's Supper. Paul focuses the correction on the need for a proper worshipful attitude at this celebration, rather than on correct theology or right procedure.

TEACHING OBJECTIVE: To worship God with the correct attitude through partaking of the Lord's Supper.

DISCUSSION IDEAS:
Plan to use the last half of your discussion time to observe the Lord's Supper. Discuss the mechanics of doing this with your pastor so appropriate preparations can be made.

1. In what circumstances is the Lord's Supper especially meaningful for you?

2. Meetings can be beneficial, neutral, or harmful. To make meetings beneficial, what should church leader's do? What should you do?

3. What kinds of divisions do not harm worship?

4. Make a list of these joyful aspects and remind the group of them during your celebration of the Lord's Supper.

5. Note that Paul is warning against an unworthy manner, not an unworthy participant.

6. Incorporate ideas from this question in your celebration.

7. Instead of discussing this question, incorporate the

answers into your worship time by having each person read their addresses to God after partaking of the elements.

SUMMARY: Jesus Christ instituted the ritual of bread and wine as a proclamation of His death and all it accomplished.

The Resurrection

1 Corinthians 15

PERSPECTIVE: Some contend that 1 Corinthians actually consists of two or more letters because it lacks a single unifying theme. It reads more like a series of essays than a letter. This chapter is perhaps the definitive essay on the Resurrection. It deals with its importance, proofs, implications, manner of occurrence, and applications for life.

The Resurrection is the cornerstone of all joyous celebration and worship, for without it Christ died in vain and "we are to be pitied more than all men." But with it we shout, "But thanks be to God! He gives us the victory through our Lord Jesus Christ!"

TEACHING OBJECTIVE: To celebrate the resurrection as Christ's victory over death and the foundation of our faith.

DISCUSSION IDEAS:
1. Do you think there is sufficient evidence to legally prove that Jesus rose from the dead in a court of law? Explain.

2. If Jesus had not been raised, would God still be worthy of worship? Would you personally worship Him?

3. Our future body will be imperishable, glorified, powerful, and spiritual. Can we apply these same terms to our worship? Explain.

4. Funeral services provide a unique opportunity to testify to our Lord's saving grace and work in your life because many will attend who otherwise would avoid any meeting with spiritual overtones. Challenge the members of your group to write a letter testifying of the resurrection power to be read as part of their funerals.

5,6. Have the best public speaker in your group read verses 50-58 aloud while the others contemplate the Resurrection worshipfully. Then encourage the group to read their praises to God from question 6 and to express other thoughts and feelings in prayer, recited verses, psalms, poetry, song, or any other appropriate manner.

SUMMARY: The final proof that Jesus is Lord is the Resurrection, for in it He defeated the one power that no one else is able to overcome: death.

By Yourself

Psalm 101

PERSPECTIVE: The Old Covenant prescribed the location for worship: the temple. It prescribed a method of worship: the Law. And it prescribed mediators for worship: the Levitical priests. But now "you are a chosen people, a royal priesthood, a holy nation, a people belonging to God, that you may declare the praises of him who called you out of darkness into his wonderful light" (1 Peter 2:9). Thus you, as an individual, can worship God any place, any time, with your choice of format, and it is acceptable to God.

TEACHING OBJECTIVE: To utilize our priesthood and independently worship God daily.

DISCUSSION IDEAS:
1. What are some of the major benefits of worshiping God by yourself?

2. What is the difference between being sinless and blameless? What should a person who doesn't feel blameless do?

3. Do you think David was speaking literally?

   Promotion, popularity, money, beauty, and accomplishment are common goals people set their eyes on. When and how do these things become vile?

4. In completing this exercise, each person has written a short psalm of praise. Give everyone an opportunity to present it to God in a time of worship.

5. Who are the people who encourage and help you to worship God? How do they do this?

7. Challenge the group to plan for an extended time of worship. Discuss some ideas for making that time most beneficial.

8. Arrange for several members of your group to present

some innovative ideas for personal worship. After each presentation, spend two or three minutes in individual worship, using the idea presented.

SUMMARY: Like David, you can worship God in your house.

In the Congregation
Romans 15:5-13

PERSPECTIVE: The book of Romans can be summarized in three words: God saves sinners. It is Paul's great thesis on salvation by grace through faith. This salvation grants us reconciliation with God (justification) that is intended to lead us to practical holiness of life (sanctification).

As in most of his letters, Paul establishes the truth of his thesis in the first half of Romans and applies it to life in the second half. The last major application given in this letter is from the study passage.

TEACHING OBJECTIVE: To congregate regularly with other believers for worship and praise.

DISCUSSION IDEAS:
1. What are some evidences of a spirit of unity and of a lack of it? What are essential ingredients of a spirit of unity?

   Expressing appreciation for one another can foster a spirit of unity. For each person in your group, have two others tell one thing they appreciate about that person. Use some form of random selection, such as drawing names from a hat, to determine who will express appreciation for whom.

2. What are the major benefits you personally experience from worshiping with others?

3. Describe the kind of person that Jesus did not accept. Which of the adjectives used to describe this person apply to you, too? Does thinking about this help you move toward accepting others?

4. How do you react when you discover that an activity you rate as a 1 someone else rates as a 10?

5. What are some forms of praising God that can be used in a

145

congregational worship service? Use some of the forms suggested to spend time together praising God.

SUMMARY: Congregational worship that glorifies God requires a spirit of unity and acceptance.

With the Heavenly Host

Revelation 4:1-5:14

PERSPECTIVE: No book of the Bible has spawned more debate than the book of Revelation. With all of its imagery, there is room for a multitude of interpretations. But one concept from this book seems abundantly clear: the Triune God is to be praised and worshiped. In this passage, no fewer than five assemblages from heaven and earth offer praise and adoration to God.

TEACHING OBJECTIVE: To see through the eyes of faith the vast and varied host that joins us when we worship God.

DISCUSSION IDEAS:
1. What do you think is the most attractive aspect of heaven? Do you think some people would not find heaven attractive? Explain.

2. Figurative language is often used for an emotional impact instead of technical accuracy. What emotions do you experience when you read this passage?

3. Have the group use their responses in a time of worth-ship by having each person fill in the blanks: "You are worthy, Lord, of . . . for. . . ."

5. The heavenly host numbers more than 100 million (Revelation 5:11). What happens inside you when you are in a large crowd that is unified in heart and purpose?

6. Jesus is called both a lion and a lamb in this passage. Which of these figures prompts you to a greater sense of worship? Why?

7. Make a list of suggestions to submit to church leaders.

   Encourage group members to use some of the ideas in their personal worship over the next week and to be prepared to relate their experiences in doing so.

147

SUMMARY: The heavenly host never stop worshiping God, and recognizing their companionship can enhance your worship experience.

In Prayer

Psalm 138

PERSPECTIVE: Nothing is more natural to worship than prayer. It is a normal response of the heart of all those who have a sense of awe of God. In prayer we talk to God and tell Him how we feel about Him. We lift our voices in praise and adoration. We express love and appreciation. The tradition of bowing in prayer is a sign of humility and unworthiness as we approach the One who is all worthy.

TEACHING OBJECTIVE: To maintain a continual prayer focus on thanksgiving, praise, and adoration before God.

DISCUSSION IDEAS:

1. What puts you in a positive mood for worship?

2. How do you interpret the phrase, "before the gods" in this verse?

3. After a brief discussion of ideas, spend two or three minutes using the ideas for each type of prayer.

5. What can help us identify God's specific purpose for each one of us?

   If people in your group do not have a grasp on God's purposes for their lives, ask the rest of the group to tell what they think might be God's purpose for each one.

7. After people have had an opportunity to express their thoughts from this exercise, have some of them read the psalm they chose out loud as a group prayer of worship.

SUMMARY: Use prayer in worship to praise God, to repeat His mighty deeds, to express your love and devotion, and to talk to Him heart to heart.

With Truth

Psalm 119:97-176

PERSPECTIVE: Psalm 119 is the longest chapter in the Bible. It extols the benefits of knowing and applying the truth of God's Word. Most of the verses are addressed to God Himself and are praises to Him. So this psalm gives us many reasons for incorporating God's Word into worship and gives us an example of doing it.

TEACHING OBJECTIVE: To obey God's truth in worship and in life.

DISCUSSION IDEAS:

1. How do you think studying the Scriptures relates to using the Word in worship?

2. What are other results of not obeying the truth?

3. If there are so many benefits of obeying God's Word, why do so many fail to do it?

4. Have those who tell of a creative way of using God's Word in worship instruct the group on how to do it. Then spend a few minutes using that method in group worship.

5. Is it possible to worship in spirit but not in truth? In truth but not in spirit?

    If someone considers something important, is it important for that person?

6. Ask your group first to list some of your worship traditions and then to evaluate them by the Word.

SUMMARY: God's Word teaches us to worship Him, gives us an example of worship, and is a proper focus of our worship.

CELEBRATE!—CHAPTER 12
With Music

Psalm 33

PERSPECTIVE: There is an interesting parallel between being drunk and being filled with the Holy Spirit. At Pentecost the believers were filled with the Holy Spirit, and onlookers thought they were drunk. Paul also draws a comparison between the two states in Ephesians 5:18. "Do not get drunk on wine. . . . Instead, be filled with the Spirit."

One of the most common reactions to alcohol is singing. The motivation is different and the songs are usually different, but singing also seems to befit those who are rightly related to God. Instrumental music is equally appropriate.

TEACHING OBJECTIVE: To use music appropriately and correctly in private and corporate worship.

DISCUSSION IDEAS:

1. Why do many people fail to sing jubilantly at worship services? What ideas do you have to help them enjoy singing and participate more enthusiastically?

3. Can you think of any hymns that are not consistent with the teachings of Scripture?

4. What do you think parents can and should do to regulate the musical diet of their children? How would you advise parents?

5. Have a time of worship with music by singing one verse of two or three songs from each of the six categories.

6. What was the best experience you had this week in musical worship?

7. Record the best ideas from your group and submit them to the leaders of your church.

SUMMARY: Singing songs, playing instruments, shouting, and making a joyful noise are all appropriate for worship.

Churches Alive!

This study is just one item in a wide range of small group material authored by Churches Alive. Continue your study with other books in this series.

Churches Alive has local representatives who provide their own living expenses to serve you at your church. On-site support and training conferences will develop commitment and vision in group leaders. Our experienced staff can help you develop leaders, enrich your groups, and reach out to others.

Conferences and Support Services

A Pastor's Perspective:

"Churches Alive was a tremendous help to us when we were getting started in our discipleship ministry. We had to make a choice—either try to learn ourselves and make a lot of mistakes, or get some help and minimize mistakes. Their careful but goal-oriented approach helps any church build a solid, perpetuating ministry."

Churches Alive!
600 Meridian Avenue
Suite 200
San Jose, CA 95126
(408) 294-6000
(408) 294-6029 FAX

Conferences

Designed to strengthen the effectiveness of your leaders, our conferences and seminars range from one to four days. Most are taught by Churches Alive staff and local pastors. In addition, we arrange special seminars in your church to encourage people in your church to study the Bible.

Support Services

In dozens of denominations, our staff helps churches large and small. We can help you evaluate, plan, train leaders, and expand your small groups. Invite a Churches Alive representative to explore small group discipleship at your church.

Call 1-800-755-3787